Service Management Process Maps – Your route to service excellence

Colophon

Title:	Service Management Process Maps – Your route to service excellence
Design and concepts:	Brian Johnson
Editors:	Nancy Hinich John Kampman Robert Sterbens Peter Waterhouse Gary West Jayne Wilkinson Inform-IT
Publisher:	Van Haren Publishing, Zaltbommel, www.vanharen.net
ISBN(13):	9789087530440
Edition:	First edition, first impression, April 2007
Design and Layout:	CO2 Premedia, Amersfoort – NL
Printer:	Wilco, Amersfoort – NL

For further enquiries about Van Haren Publishing, please send an e-mail to: info@vanharen.net

Service Management Process Maps –
Your route to service excellence

Foreword

The greatest challenge faced by most IT organizations today is performing a balancing act, between continuing to keep IT running while also enhancing the quality of their service and responding with greater agility to ever-changing business needs. These various pressures have led to the IT industry's current fascination with process re-engineering and ITIL. Unfortunately, for the purposes of day-to-day practical application, ITIL was intentionally designed as a high-level framework, describing 'what' should be done, without providing enough prescriptive guidance on 'how' to go about doing it.

This lack of prescriptive guidance presents IT organizations with a frustrating conundrum: the seemingly elementary questions of where to start, how much needs to be implemented, and how to measure success. The authors of this book understand these issues all too well. To help readers get started, they present innovative concepts about the 'on and off ramps' of the IT service management processes. The useful, widely understood metaphor of a mass transit map helps to make individual processes and their discrete intersections clearer and easier to follow. The authors also offer illumination on the question of how participants can go about rationalizing a process program in context with changes that are incremental, evolutionary or revolutionary. The authors caution against taking on a project that is too large in scope, such as working on all 10 of the core service support and service delivery processes at once. Instead, they focus attention on common groupings and achievable, holistic planning. This book will help its readers rethink their ITIL implementations, as a multi-phased effort, and assist them with keeping them closely focused at first on pain points that, if addressed, could potentially deliver measurable benefits within a reasonable span of time. This emphasis on a close focus may also reduce the temptation that besets most companies engaged in process refinement — which is to rush into developing overly complex process workflows. This book is a map that will help to get its lost or confused readers through the 'station', back on the 'track' and heading in the right 'direction'.

Pete McGarahan, Chairman, ITIM Strategic Advisory Board

Acknowledgements

Several people have been instrumental in allowing this project to be completed. We would like to thank especially Brian Johnson, VP and WW ITIL Practice Manager, Technical Services, CA Inc. (United Kingdom), who was the initial instigator, had conceptualized and visualized the ITIL framework and its interdependent ITSM processes in the form of a easy to navigate subway map, and early on provided advice and encouragement. We would also like to thank Peter Waterhouse, Director, Brand, CA Inc. (Australia), for without his commitment, leadership and willingness to co-ordinate the efforts of CA ITIL experts worldwide, this book would not have been possible.

Design and Concepts: Brian Johnson

Editors   Nancy Hinich
                         John Kampman
                         Robert Sterbens
                         Peter Waterhouse
                         Gary West
                         Jayne Wilkinson
                         Inform-IT

Authors   Peter Doherty
                         Nancy Hinich
                         Brian Johnson
                         John Kampman
                         Randal Locke
                         Olivier Martin
                         Takashi Maeda
                         Alan Nance
                         Jesús Rivas
                         Atanu Roy
                         Robert Sterbens
                         Marvin Waschke
                         Pete Waterhouse
                         Paul Wilkinson

Contents

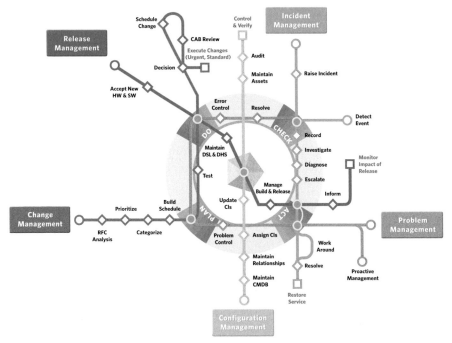

Service Support Subway Map

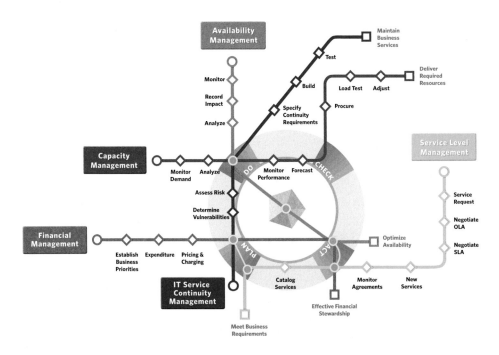

Service Delivery Subway Map

Introduction

The London Underground

In the 1850s, the engineers of Victorian London designed the immense underground system for mass transport of the population around the capital. With a myriad of possible entry and exit points, they did not initially consider how to explain to putative customers the ways in which they were to get from point A to point B.

They designed a complex series of linked tracks, with careful consideration being given to minor details such as making sure that tunnels did not sit directly above other tunnels, it being a good idea that a collapse was avoided. They ensured that the even more complex above-ground urban terrain did not complicate their selected solutions and they made sure that if you needed to ascend or descend in order to use their services, the underground tracks could be reached by elevators to facilitate changing both direction and altitude, without too much inconvenience.

Further, the whole was always perceived to be an integrated piece, with numerous moving parts that needed to be co-ordinated and managed, because it was, well, complicated. And it would most likely grow, sometimes predictably, to accommodate demographics and, sometimes, simply because someone wanted to transport people to a large dome built for the millennium.

The London Underground now covers 253 miles and has 275 stations; and it is both above and below ground as well as being multi-level under the ground. Rather cleverly, a 'circle' line was designed and built to ensure that many of the main tracks were linked at multiple access points. And even more cleverly, a map was later produced (Harry Beck designed the map in 1933) that simplified the underground by ignoring the multiple levels and, indeed, largely ignoring the above ground topography. Essentially it took a three dimensional model and collapsed the view to two dimensions; it also abstracted the reality of the topography that was its raison d'etre to a form that was simple to construct, display and understand.

The IT Underground

Of course, IT is much more complex than the London Underground, and IT Service Management (ITSM) is even more complex, otherwise we would not have warehouses full of books created to sustain the complexity and the ability of the gifted few to understand it. IT that is.

If we suspend our self-sustained mythology for a moment or two, it is possible to consider that the analogy of the map of the London Underground, or the New York subway or the Paris Metro - whatever - can be applied to good effect in ITSM.

Take the processes of the IT Infrastructure Library (ITIL) for example, the Rubik's Cube of the twenty-first century. The complexity of ITIL is legendary, as are the select few who can help you to understand it and explain it for you, the uninitiated or worse, the uncertified (those who have yet to receive ITIL Practitioner or Master Certification). Fortunately by learning from the genius who simplified the engineering of the subway systems, it is possible to explain ITIL in a rational manner, in a way that has depth and that shows the most important interfaces, yet can be understood by the average person. If you can read a subway map you can understand the complexities of ITIL; bad news for the guru's but good for the rest of us.

ITIL is simple
There are really only two concepts that you need to get straight to understand how ITSM and ITIL can be explained in the same way as a nineteenth century engineering paradigm. First, all best practices are based on the Deming Quality Cycle of 'Plan Do Check Act' (P-D-C-A); all focus on gradual continuous improvement using this approach. The second is that you need a means to assess and measure improvement and in IT the most common way is to assess levels of maturity using either the capability maturity model (CMM) developed by Carnegie Mellon University, or one of the models based on that first design that uses the same principles.

And guess what? The 'new' ITIL (version 3) is going to be based on the Deming principles and levels of maturity.

Thus, the content discussed in this book is as relevant for the future as for the present. We are simplifying ITIL only in terms of abstracting a sensible, easy to understand and fundamentally sound mapping. The major engineering (ie the topography and the tunnels: in IT, the business landscape is the topography and the IT is the tunnels) continue to exist and are addressed using the maps as the guide.

We have created two maps:

- a service delivery subway map
- a service support subway map

We could have (as with the London Underground), collapsed these into a single view; why have we chosen not to do this?

The analogy in context

The business landscape is much more complicated than the IT tunnels, and the majority of business people want to discuss concepts such as procurement, information systems (applications), knowledge, governance, security, risk and management of programs. These concepts are part of every track, though in IT, the most popular discussions revolve around the groups of processes discussed in the ITIL service support and service delivery volumes.

We have separated the maps in order to more easily represent in individual maps the P-D-C-A cycle and the relationship between the most common groupings. Another reason is then to illustrate how increased organizational maturity 'levels' are achieved by planning holistically, so that operational, tactical and strategic processes are discussed at the outset, and proper thought is given to how the 'levels' will be achieved and the goals of both business and IT considered for the programs/projects. Service delivery processes (and, of course, the map) are much more focused on business issues than service support; thus it makes sense to separate the activities for a different type of discussion.

The P-D-C-A cycle becomes in effect, our 'circle line' (see figure 1.1) and the ITIL process 'tracks' are located in the most appropriate location to illustrate major interfaces and 'direction'. ITIL is not definitive (nor can it be, because of the broad nature of the guidance), but it can be illustrated in a manner that enables us to think about the big picture and not to get distracted by the tunnels, the procedures, the software and organizational change that needs to be addressed to make it all work.

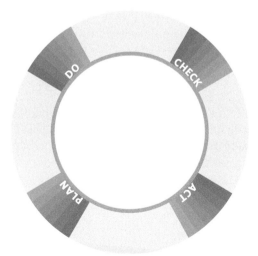

Figure 1.1 Deming's Continuous Improvement Cycle

If, for sake of illustration, we select a 'track' that we feel is most important to our organization, the P-D-C-A 'stations' also serve as reference points for us to ascend (or descend) to another track to think about the planning implications or perhaps to review issues of a decision to implement our selection in isolation from other 'tracks'.

An example
The most commonly 'implemented' ITIL process is Incident Management. The track shows the most important sub processes, or stations, but does not attempt to over- elaborate by contextualizing either the business issues or the IT software support. It is positioned at the 'check/act' point of the cycle for only one reason. It is always described as the process that acts as the check on all of the other processes. Of course, the major purpose is to get things up and running for the user, so it makes sense that the 'act' station is also highlighted.

ITSM is mature in the market place, and most organizations will want to link Incident and Problem Management. So the problem track starts = out at the 'act' corner but because it is a process focused on eradicating problems, it proceeds right through the P-D-C-A cycle. Why? Well, because we want to start connecting the stations logically in a manner that provides the opportunity to consider other processes at the right time. So we next consider Change Management. Much more aligned to planning and, when linked to the Release Management process, we start to create the bigger picture of the change lifecycle.

And what do we need to hold things together: something that drives right through the heart of the cycles of P-D-C-A and change? We need the Configuration Management process.

Incidentally (if you will excuse the pun), why do you suppose the Release Management track ends up near the start of the Incident track? Yes, because every time a change is released, we see more incidents---unless of course, you are pulling together an ITIL based process improvement project!

The Service Support and Service Delivery subways are expanded upon next. And then we will take you along each of the tracks in more detail. We will be covering the tracks as a process concern, not as a technology concern.

1 Service Management Process Maps: Select Your Route to ITIL® Best Practice

1.1 ITIL Revisited

ITIL can be applied in any organization, regardless of size, type and structure. Like many business quality initiatives, it is based on the principles of W. Edwards Deming, an American statistician who argued that supplying products or services requires activities, and the quality of a service depends upon the way activities are organized. Deming's Quality Cycle (figure 1.1) proposed a system of continuous improvement, with the appropriate levels of quality delivered by adhering to the following steps:

- **PLAN** - design or revise components to improve results
- **DO** - ensure the plan is implemented
- **CHECK** - determine if the activities achieved the expected results
- **ACT** - adjust the plan based on results gathered during the check phase

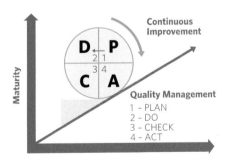

Figure 1.1 Deming's Quality Circle

ITIL provides information on numerous ITSM best practices, including detailed process activity requirements, procedures, roles and responsibilities which can be tailored to any organization. These practices have been defined as a series of processes covering the major activities that should be provided by any IT organization. These processes are grouped into two major areas: Service Support and Service Delivery.

1.1.1 Service Support

This describes how customers can access the appropriate IT services to support their business. In many ways, Service Support describes the day-to-day operational foundation services used to meet customer needs (see figure 1.2).

Service Support processes include:
- **Incident Management** - to restore services with minimal business disruption
- **Problem Management** - to minimize the adverse affect of IT problems
- **Change Management** - to determine required changes, and implement with minimum adverse impact
- **Configuration Management** - to identify, control and verify configurations supporting IT services
- **Release Management** - to ensure that only tested and correct versions of hardware and software are provided
- **Service Desk (function) -** to provide a single, central point of contact for all users of IT within the organization; at a minimum, the service desk function handles all incidents, service and changes requests and provides an interface to all of the other service support processes

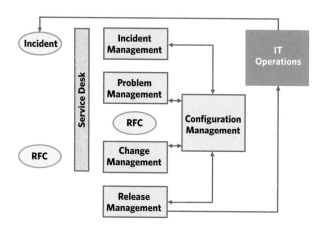

Figure 1.2 Service Support Processes

1.1.2 Service Delivery

This describes the five processes that help IT organizations to deliver the requisite business services (figure 1.3). Transformational in nature, the processes are concerned with the planning and delivery of quality IT services. Service Delivery processes include:

- **Service Level Management** - to make service agreements with customers about IT services, and to implement and monitor those agreements
- **Availability Management** - to ensure the appropriate level of resources to support the availability of IT services
- **Financial Management for IT Services** - to provide cost effective control over IT assets and resources

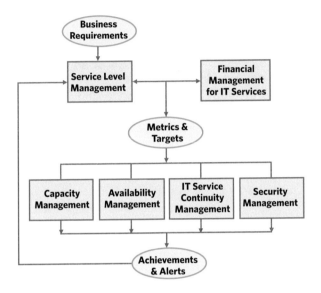

Figure 1.3 Service Delivery Processes

- **Capacity Management** - to ensure that adequate capacity is available to meet business requirements, balancing supply with demand
- **IT Service Continuity Management** - to address the preparation and planning of disaster recovery procedures for IT services

1.2 The ITIL Journey

Many IT organizations are looking to ITIL as a solution without really understanding the problem. A common misconception is that ITIL can be implemented like any technology or application. This may be due, in part, to the technology-centric nature of the acronym ITIL, or process names themselves (for example, availability management).

ITIL is a catalyst to change the way an organization operates. Traditionally, IT has operated in functional silos with separate goals and objectives. But in today's environment, IT must become a service oriented culture, where cross-functional teams are unified in the common pursuit of service excellence. ITIL is founded on this premise, but ITIL itself cannot change an IT organizational culture. Senior IT and business management must also endorse ITIL. Endorsement from the business is particularly critical for success since ITIL is not an IT project, but a program focused on increasing efficiency and aligning business and IT processes. Confining ITIL discussions to the IT department is a recipe for disaster, since there will be no mutual agreement on overall business objectives and deliverables. In addition, the optimization of many ITIL processes, such as Service Level Management (SLM), is dependent on the collaboration between business and IT.

1.3 ITIL—Descriptive –v- Prescriptive

For the most part, ITIL describes what needs to be done to improve service without explaining how to do it. Simply having ITIL documentation describe repeatable management processes will not translate into actual service improvement. Organizations need to take the descriptive elements of ITIL and prescribe the actionable guidelines and blueprints to put ITIL theory into IT Service Management best practice. In many ways, navigating ITIL can be like trying to find your way across an urban underground transit system using a multi-volume street atlas. You know where you want to go, but too much detail and superfluous information will not help you to optimize your journey, especially if you have to change lines to arrive at your destination.

1.4 A Lesson from Engineering History

London's massive underground transit system is a marvel of engineering. It comprises a series of linked tracks, with careful consideration given to the placement of junctions that would facilitate optimum transportation. Much like the ITIL framework, the whole was perceived to be an integrated piece, with many moving parts to co-ordinate and manage.

For the benefit of travelers a single map of the entire underground system was produced. It presented every track and junction point in a clear and simple way, ignoring irrelevant details and enabling everyone to easily navigate their way across the network.

1.5 Continuous Improvement

Many organizations start their ITIL journey with a narrow focus on Service Support processes. But planning to implement just one process without thinking of the impact on other processes will lead to 'continuously revisiting' instead of 'continuously improving'. For example, ideal Incident

Management is difficult to achieve if most incidents are the result of unauthorized change activities. In this case, a journey towards improvement in one process will involve many side-routes.

ITIL implementations should be looked at holistically, using the principles of Deming to drive and ensure that continuous improvement is always being applied. The relationships between ITIL processes must always be considered with rigorous attention to their place and role in a continuous improvement cycle of PLAN, DO, CHECK and ACT.

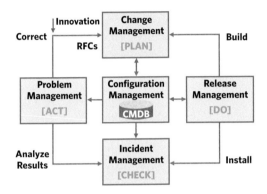

Figure 1.4 Continuous Process Improvement

Consider figure 1.4, and the relationship between Change, Release, Incident and Problem Management. Here we can see that Change Management should be considered as a **PLAN**ning process, with the specific goal of introducing IT improvements, often based on business imperatives. Release Management implements the changes (a **DO** activity), and Incident Management is the **CHECK**ing process, determining if the activities achieved the desired results, by monitoring any incidents introduced as a result of the change. If the results were not achieved then Problem Management, the **ACT**ing process is engaged to perform a root cause analysis to determine the true cause and appropriate corrective action. This output is fed into the planning process and starts another continuous improvement cycle.

Problem Management finds the root-cause of any problems introduced and feeds this back, often in the form of Request for Changes (RFC) to the Change Management process. Thus, the continuous improvement cycle starts again.

1.6 The ITSM Subway or Underground System

Of course, IT Service Management is far more complex than an underground transit system. However, the analogy of a transit map - be it

the London Underground, the New York subway system or the Paris Metro - can be applied to good effect in ITSM.
By visualizing the ITIL framework in a similar fashion to the underground transit maps, it is possible to clearly illustrate every process (or track), each activity (or station) and the key interfaces (junctions) that are needed to chart and navigate a journey of continuous IT service improvement.

1.7 ITIL is Simple (Really, it is)

Two basic concepts explain how ITSM and ITIL can be viewed in the same way as a subway system or underground transport map. First, as discussed above, best practices - including ITIL - are based on the Deming Quality Cycle of 'Plan-Do-Check-Act, and focus on gradual continuous improvement using this approach. The second is as a means to assess and measure improvement.

In IT, the most common method is to assess levels of maturity using a capability maturity model (CMM) analogous to the ones developed by Carnegie Mellon University or one of the models based on similar principles. This approach is relevant for the current and the next release of ITIL, which will continue to be based on the Deming principles and levels of maturity.

2 Service Support and Service Delivery - An Introduction

2.1 Service Support

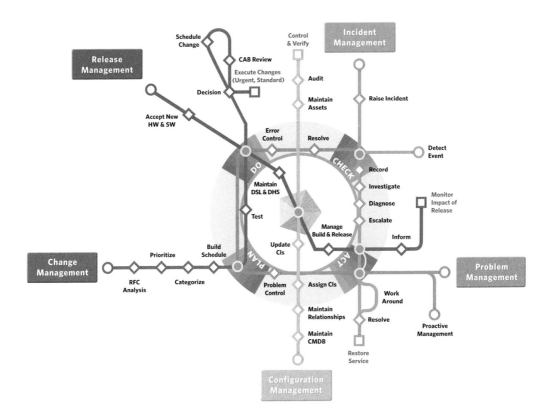

Figure 2.1 Service Support Subway Map

Service Support is often seen as the starting point for an ITIL implementation program (see figure 2.1). Although there is no right or wrong place to start, there are common reasons for beginning with the Service Support subway tracks. Just ask yourself the question 'How can I determine the cost of Service provisioning and maintenance without knowing what I have now and how I perform currently? How do I support the business and how do I put things into perspective? Above all, how do I take control?' During the early days of ITIL, it was 'cool' to have implemented a Service Desk and then to tell everybody, 'yes, we have an Incident Management process!' In reality, the process was not there at all, but rather, it was used as a placeholder; people eventually learned that the service desk was, in fact, a function and the activities of taking calls and follow-up activities end-to-end was the process. Shortly after that, there was more thinking around the support processes and new emphasis on streamlining with the related business functions; even so, this was fragmented and reactive.

This reactive and isolated way of working was exactly the reason why many Best Practice implementation programs did not succeed; many IT organizations today are also compartmentalized into silos   Incidents were considered managed, but there was no real connection to potential problems and there was no connection to the Change Management process or Release Management side of the house. By working in these process silos, the business organization was not benefiting from the full extent of a Best Practices Implementation.

The Service Support chapters or 'process tracks' examine the 'Big Picture', including natural integration points for:

- Service Desk
- Incident Management
- Problem Management
- Change Management
- Configuration Management
- Release Management

Let's start with a ticket on the ITIL Service Support subway (figure 2.1) in order to take a closer look at Service Support and how an organization might benefit from the flexibility of the tracks (process) working together, and automation of the tracks. Each individual track will be discussed in detail in following separate chapters. Each chapter focuses on a specific process or 'subway line' and the key activities or 'stops' along the track are discussed in relation to other key processes or 'transfer stations' with the end goal of optimizing your journey through automation.

2.2 Service Delivery

Service Delivery is often seen as the most difficult part of the ITIL journey. As with Service Support, there is no right or wrong place to start, but much more so than with Service Support, Service Delivery subway 'tracks' (process) focus on business issues. Ask yourself a second time the questions 'How can I determine the cost of service provisioning and maintenance without knowing what I have now and how I perform currently? How do I deliver value-add services to the business, and how do I put the business' needs into perspective? Above all, how do I take control?'

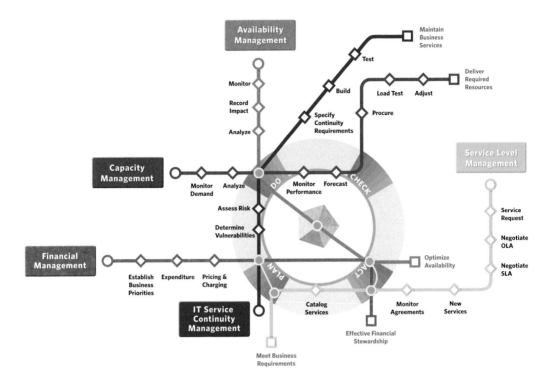

Figure 2.2 Service Delivery Subway Map

While the processes within Service Support are important to underpin IT service provisioning the 'difficult', Service Delivery processes are customer facing and, when managed coherently, have a much wider impact on the user community. The impact, or risk as some people would say, needs to be carefully considered as you work through implementing Service Delivery processes. Implementing Service Delivery processes needs to be carefully planned so as not to impact your business whilst being deployed.

By working solely on IT facing tracks, the business organization was not benefiting from the full extent of a Best Practices Implementation and often questioned—or even cut-off—the investment. The Service Delivery tracks are the ones that attract the business to invest in the tunnels! They are also the processes that need 'buy in' from everyone within the organization, as to implement these processes without the buy in will limit the return on investment you receive, and will also increase the risk to your organization. Buy in or 'cultural change' is a key component to the planning for the ITIL process roll out.

The Service Delivery chapters or 'process tracks' examine the 'Big Picture', including natural integration points for:

- IT Service Continuity Management
- Service Level Management
- Capacity Management
- Configuration Management
- Financial Management
- Availability Management

We have included Configuration Management here, although it is a Service Support process because it is the integration point for all processes; this is another reason to ensure that ITIL planning is coherent and all-embracing, irrespective of the timescale over which embedding is planned.

Let's purchase another ticket on the ITIL Service Delivery (figure 2.2) subway in order to take a closer look at Service Delivery and how an organization might benefit from the flexibility of the processes working harmoniously, and automation of those processes. Once again, each individual track will be discussed in detail in the separate chapters following this section. Each chapter focuses on a specific process or 'subway line' and the key activities or 'stops' along the track are discussed in relation to other key processes or 'transfer stations', with the end goal of optimizing your journey through automation.

Ok; so Service Delivery can be considered the 'visible' side of ITIL to the business. This is not to say that the Service Delivery lines should be implemented prior to the Service Support tracks being navigated; remember there is no 'right' place to start; you just have to start.

Most organizations that are traveling along the Service Delivery lines generally are considered to be more 'mature' and have finished constructing their support lines, or, more accurately, will have constructed the ones appropriate to them, or have recognized delivery issues to the business as critical. In any instance, the organization is generally at a higher level of maturity in its planning to achieve business goals, and has planned for the natural integration points and automations between the processes.

Service Delivery is characterized by a significant shift in focus that brings the business to the fore. So what are the characteristics of the journey that need to be highlighted?

Plan
Each Service Delivery chapter provides you with an overview of the key activities or 'stops' along the Service Delivery lines through the 'Plan Do Check Act' cycle, and discusses optimization through automation and integration along the way. And though it is true to say that planning is

crucial for any ITIL process, and we hope that we have at least illustrated that, the support processes must be planned as a coherent structure; failure to co-ordinate plans for capacity, financial, service, IT service continuity and availability processes will lead to a messy, expensive and unreliable provision of IT services.

The ITIL books recommend a capacity plan, an availability plan, an IT Service Continuity Management (ITSCM) plan for … you get the idea. Nowhere else is the planning process more overt or visible and nowhere else is planning more neglected too. Program management is the co-ordination of a number of projects that, if managed together, is more beneficial than if the projects were separately managed. Service Delivery is, or should be, a program. Once more we are not telling you to where to start or which tracks to plan, we are telling you to consider the entire map so that the tracks are planned intelligently and coherently.

When the planners of the Tube looked at the topography of London, do you imagine they allowed individual tracks to be planned in isolation? Or take a look at the incredibly convoluted, but eminently navigable Tokyo Metro. Planning is the key activity.

It is important to consider how you are going to ensure that your organization travels this journey with you. There is no point in building an infrastructure that no one is going to use. The Tube in London would not have been successful if there were no customers. And how do you retain customers? Or in this case, how do you maintain adherence to process design in order to maintain efficiency; it is very common to find that new processes are adhered to for a time and then the old ways - whatever they may be - start to re-emerge. It is human nature that, when the road gets bumpy or too hard, those who are uncommitted to the journey will find ways to get off the train. Organizations need to show 'successes' along the journey to maintain interest and to show return on investment at different stops. Ensure that part of your planning addresses cultural issues and fully addresses how you intend to maintain processes and, of course, to continuously improve the processes.

Consider also the communications that will be needed to ensure that your program does not run into problems with regard to dependencies either going unrecognized or ignored. Without knowing the proposed content of availability plans how can the capacity manager plan to support the future business? Or how will the financial manager know the projected costs and charges that need to be budgeted? And crucially, how will IT Service Continuity Management (ITSCM) ever be effective without knowledge of what can be spent and where, and what are the service levels required in the event of a disaster causing a wholesale infrastructure move to a new hot-standby site? And these are just some of the most obvious pitfalls.

And this is only the beginning of the multiple journeys you can take, because holistic planning of change processes and the all-encompassing Configuration Management Database (CMDB) and its interfaces need also to be considered.

This actually leads us to planning the infamous word 'success'. We mentioned maintaining interest and showing successes/return on investment. It is important that you consider how you are going to communicate successes to your organization - and when. Silence is the fastest and most efficient way to end the ITIL journey; sometimes it seems to end it before it has begun. Ensure that your Communication Plan is developed with your organization structure, culture and goals in mind.

Do
Acting on the planning process, embedding changes and ideas all come under this heading. One piece of advice in this section, ensure that you 'do' all of the things that you have planned. Organizations often lay out plans and then don't follow them. Key to your success is actually following the plan that you laid out.

Should the Plan need to change throughout the journey (which is entirely likely), then ensure that you communicate both the changes to the plan and the changes to the actions that you had originally identified to the organization.

Doing is, in many cases, synonymous with embedding. And in order to embed new processes you need to have a metrics framework in place that allows you to intervene if needed, and to direct, validate or justify whatever it is that you are doing. Metrics may be very similar across the individual tracks, though it is recommended that when thinking about delivery metrics, the goals should be elevated in line with business goals. For example, if you need an Availability Management goal checkmark, make sure it is not focused on the IT networks but on availability of critical applications to the users.

Embedding SLM is also going to be different to embedding, say, Financial Management. In the first case the focus should be on being the customer advocate within IT services, as well as the barometer of customer satisfaction, whereas the latter will be ensuring that projected costs and charges are in line with reality. Of course, in the support processes the action of doing tends to be IT centric, but the impact of the changes is felt at the delivery end - if system capacity incidents are causing downtime, then who will be taking action to reduce demand?

Check
As with all plans, the review (either at the checkpoints or at Post Implementation Review), is essential to allow for improvements or changes

in direction, or even a complete rethink. Once again, consider why we measure anything: to intervene if needed, and to direct, validate or justify whatever it is that you are doing. Now is the time to look at what has been happening with your program and provide evidence that it is still on track, and still going in the right direction.

Keep in mind that continuous improvement, however incremental and however small, is the goal of any best practice framework. You may discover that the program is too big, or that it was too expensive or perhaps too ambitious. Your measurement framework will be the pointer to what you need to do to either get things 'back on track', or maybe even to go backwards! Remember that ITIL is a catalyst for change, not a goal in itself. In most ITIL projects it becomes essential at some point to re-examine the goals, to make sure that they are still in line with overall project goals and that the focus remains the business; it is very easy to hijack ITIL for IT!

Act
If changes are required during the Check process then Acting on those changes is essential. Acting on changes can be complex, as quite often you will need to identify all of the areas that are impacted by a change. In doing this analysis you may find that making the change will have a variety of impacts on your processes. Take a moment to stand back and ask if these changes are necessary at this point in your journey, or could they be set aside to be included in a future planning phase that would allow you to mitigate the risk to the business.

Acting on information in haste can lead to repenting in haste - to paraphrase an old adage. Nothing creates change like change. Taking action should be directed towards interventions (for example, Service Level Agreements, or SLAs have been breached and this is unacceptable to the business) or to direct (perhaps resources are required in a crucial area).

The actions may impact both delivery and support processes, so once more think holistically about impact.

Culture
We should not leave this section without touching on culture once more. No two organizations will have the same culture; each is different and therefore what works in each organization will also be different. Organizations will have groups within their lines of business that adopt change readily and groups that resist change. Within each of those groups you will have individuals who embrace change and those who don't. This adds a layer of complexity to the journey.

By taking the time to identify your culture and the challenges you may face in this area, this will also give you some insight into which subway stops to begin with. By boarding at a certain stop that will allow you to implement a process that is, perhaps, less intrusive to your organization, you will be able to effect the changes while mitigating the impact on your organization. Sometimes going slower and taking those small steps might be more effective than choosing a process that has a much larger impact at the beginning of your journey.

Your journey should include activities that will affect the changes you need in your organization to ensure that each step on your journey meets with success. Some organizations are turning to simulation training as an activity to effect cultural change. A number of simulation activities are available to assist organizations on this part of the journey. Good simulation activities can be customized to each organization, to ensure that those taking the journey recognize their own culture and challenges.

Communication
And to emphasize another key point, applicable to all parts of the subways: Communication is something that needs to happen constantly as your organization travels along the tracks. How you communicate and when depends very much on the organization. Organizations that communicate successfully during the journey use a variety of communication techniques, one of the most common and effective being a 'marketing' of the plans and the goals of the program. It may appear trivial, but having a modicum of fun, either with logos or events, has been demonstrated to be effective in even the most 'Ebenezer Scrooge-like' of cultures.

Take the time to develop your official 'Communication Strategy' and to develop the 'Marketing Plan' - and don't forget that these Plans are also subject to the continuous improvement cycle!

Service Support

CHAPTER **3 Service Desk Function: The Conductor of your ITSM journey**

Imagine for a moment that you are taking a journey on an underground transit system such as the London Underground, the New York Subway system or the Paris Metro. You set out to reach your destination in the fastest time possible, comfortable in the fact that a function exists to inform you of timetable changes, validate tickets, take complaints, and handle any queries. There is no doubt that urban transport systems are marvels of engineering, but it is these customer facing functions that really determine how effectively the transport system is doing its job. Without this function, the complexity which we want to shield from our customers becomes all too apparent, and the service becomes something that is scorned, criticized and often, ridiculed.

Similarly in IT, the end-user perception of the support function is a critical element in the business' determination of how well IT is doing its job. Like the transport system, IT has many touch-points with the end-user; so many that providing a single interface into the service function is critical if end-users are to enjoy a consistent and positive experience when interacting with IT.

3.1 From Help Desk to Service Desk

In ITIL, the Service Desk is regarded as a function not a process. Naturally, the Service Desk should be a place to log incidents and support the Incident Management process, but it must have a larger role than just handling incidents. As the primary interface to the end-user, the Service Desk function must also have the capability to handle a more complete set of services, such as co-ordinating change requests, proactively addressing problems, communicating service goals and achievements, and monitoring customer satisfaction.

As the role of the Service Desk expands towards being a one-stop shop for handling any type of user problem or request, then the demands on the function increase significantly. It is critical therefore that the Service Desk function provides an interface to the other ITIL processes, and can seamlessly drive workflow through automated controls. Without this, the Service Desk becomes nothing more than a centralized means of bouncing end-users around from one area to another. In such situations end-users become increasingly frustrated with the levels of service provided, and may even bypass the Service Desk function altogether by directly accessing domain level experts; hence the all-too familiar 'help-less desk' phrase. This is a situation that must be avoided at all costs because the Service Desk will have no means to measure its effectiveness, leverage shared knowledge and drive continuous improvement.

Unfortunately, many organizations regard this function as existing to perform only one task; simply there to fix user issues. This, of course, isn't incorrect, since the Service Desk's primary role is to handle activities associated with the Incident Management process. However, the mistake can arise when the organization becomes obsessed with just providing help, and not actually improving services to the end-users. Obviously, the Service Desk function exists to provide reactive help-services when things go wrong, but it also plays a critical role in driving proactive service enhancements. Take, for example, the most common request placed on the Service Desk – password resets. Research shows that as many as 25% of calls to the Service Desk are for application password resets. In a standard or traditional 'help' desk model, the end-user will call the help desk directly, and the support analyst will initiate a sequence of activities to reset the user's password. This is extremely inefficient both in terms of lost productivity and cost. In a true 'Service' desk model, the end-user would access a self-service function to automate the password reset request and would, perhaps, have access to user training for further elimination of 'how to' calls to the Service Desk. Obviously this service based approach will reduce costs by eliminating the analyst's interaction with the end-user, hence a reduction in telecom costs (call handling costs). It also improves service by standardizing a process activity. Once standardized, a process activity becomes repeatable, and repeatability drives further service improvements. It should also be noted that such methods enable the Service Desk function to report on the efficiency of other IT management practices. With the automated password reset ability, the Service Desk Manager is able to report on the number of password reset requests to the Security Manager who can use the information to help determine the efficiency of certain security policies and develop training plans for users. This is not 'help' in the traditional form, but it is improved *service*, and it is these types of capabilities that differentiate Service Desk applications.

3.2 Service Desk Goals

The primary goal of the Service Desk is to act as a central point of contact between the end-user and IT service management. The Service Desk must be equipped to handle every support need that an end-user may have of IT. On the other hand, the Service Desk function must be ready and able to proactively communicate IT activities that may affect the ability of end-users to conduct their work according to normal service levels. The Service Desk is the 'perception barometer' of IT for end-users. If an organization's end-users are dissatisfied with IT services, then the Service Desk should be the first place to look for the reasons and the answers.

Another objective of the Service Desk is to handle all incidents and requests for service. Unlike a traditional help desk system, the ITIL Service Desk function is not concerned with finding the root-cause of incidents. This is within the realm of the Problem Management process, which is initiated in response to the creation of a problem record. The Service Desk function (figure 3.1) manages incidents, acting as a front-end to the Incident Management process for rapid service restoration (see figure 3.2). As such, it is important that the Service Desk function can clearly distinguish incident from problem records. Without this capability, it becomes difficult to determine where resources should be allocated to improve each process.

Service Desk and Service Support Processes

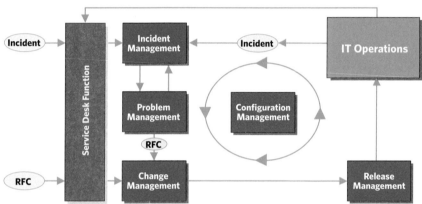

Figure 3.1 Service Desk Function handles all incidents, service and change requests and provides an interface to all of the other service support processes.

The final goal of the Service Desk is to provide an interface for the other process activities, including:

- **Change and Release Management** – acting as the central point for RFC submissions, and by co-ordinating the installation of end-user software

- **Configuration Management** – when recording incidents, the Service Desk can access the CMDB to verify the details of the end-users IT resources

- **Service Level Management** – the Service Desk can advise end-users of the IT services they are entitled to, and communicate service achievements or breaches through reporting

An optimum Service Desk should be able to support other ITIL processes and activities. As the shop-front of IT service, the Service Desk is an excellent means of maintaining contact with end-users regarding all IT services. It can also help to monitor customer satisfaction by facilitating web-based surveys.

3.3 Continuous Service Improvement

By serving as an initial point of contact and by undertaking a range of support activities for the ITIL processes, the Service Desk can significantly reduce the workload on the IT organization by intercepting issues that can be easily addressed, and by standardizing support activities through automation. When used effectively the Service Desk can accelerate success (improved service) by acting as the central mechanism that integrates with various interfacing ITIL processes. By way of illustration, consider the ITIL Service Support subway map (see figure 3.2).

As we can see, the Incident Management process starts with the recording of an incident, or the detection of a system event. In most cases the incident will be recorded by the Service Desk, and it is good practice to ensure that all incidents are recorded immediately as they are reported or detected. End-users should be able to record incidents themselves, but another good practice is to enable infrastructure management solutions to automatically record incidents when critical service thresholds are exceeded. What should be avoided, however, are situations when every single event is recorded in the Service Desk. A better approach is for management solutions to correlate multiple conditions to a single event, link this to a *business service*, and then record the incident. This avoids the situation of analysts painstakingly reviewing every system event and the Service Desk becoming overloaded.

Recent advances in Application Performance Management solutions which monitor performance from the end-user perspective (ie response times) have also enabled Service Desk incident recording to be further optimized. These solutions are proficient in detecting deviations from agreed application performance levels (even before end-users experience them), and are therefore a good way of quickly pinpointing more critical application related incidents and enabling the Service Desk to immediately notify second and third-tier support specialists.

Another extremely valuable proposition is to enable end-users to record their own incidents via self-service facilities. Building a self-service strategy can take your Service Desk to the next level of service optimization and dramatically reduce support costs. Giving the end-users a single point of contact with the Service Desk simplifies end-user communications with IT and can provide a higher level of customer service. You can also provide end-users with direct access to a broad array of support information, available knowledge, ability to reset passwords (as discussed above), system wide messaging via a bulletin board, self-training and much more. The bulletin board ability notifies end-users of current service failures within the IT organization as well as planned service outages for maintenance (contained within Change Management's Forward Schedule of Change, or FSC).

The self-service ability should allow end-users not only to create new incidents and requests for service, or to check on the status of either of these, but also to utilize support automation capabilities. Support automation is the most advanced level of self-service, and the most powerful Service Desks integrate this capability to further reduce costs through call optimization, call avoidance and call prevention. Automation optimizes the technicians contact time by automating detection, diagnosis, and repair during the live support process. Call avoidance is achieved by empowering end-users to resolve their own problems with single click access to automated problem resolution procedures. Call prevention is achieved by automatically monitoring and pushing fixes directly to end-user desktops before they are aware that a problem exists; this is extremely valuable as it drives further operational efficiencies and proactive service improvement.

Another critical aspect of the Service Desk function is to constantly monitor end-user satisfaction by providing a vehicle for continuous process improvement and ensuring customer satisfaction. Here, a survey capability, which is integrated into the Service Desk, and that uses an electronic survey system to gather customer satisfaction information based upon incidents, problems or changes in the environment, is critical for driving service improvement. Having near real-time performance information enables the Service Desk continuously to improve its perceived or actual performance.

Another key function of the Service Desk is the management of support escalations. Here it is not enough to merely supply escalation functionality. This functionality must be supplemented with a system that captures the knowledge accumulated from subject matter experts (SMEs), so that first level support analysts can resolve more incidents at first contact. Research has shown that 83% of the incidents received by a Service Desk, have been received before. Therefore, if resolution at first contact is to be a goal, a system capturing this accumulated knowledge should be strongly considered in order to aid in first contact resolution. Once an SME expert determines that there is a known error, a workaround, a bug or a fix, or that he has the knowledge to walk someone through the resolution process; this information must be captured, reviewed and published in a knowledge repository. This knowledge repository must then be made accessible by all levels in the support chain, even by the end-user via self-service (as discussed above). In this case, it is important that the Service Desk function can segment knowledge so that end-users only have access to those documents that are appropriate and end-user friendly. Another function is communication across all levels of support, managing the incidents, problem and changes themselves. Each level of technician should have a mechanism in which to record everything that they are doing within that call and it should be contained with the single application. If this is performed effectively, then the first level technician or end-user has the capability to understand the exact status of the incident at all times.

The following is an example of the effective use of status information:

- The end-user calls the Service Desk and speaks with a Level 1 support technician. An incident record is created and assigned an 'Open' status if the support analyst cannot resolve the incident at first contact.
- The incident is transferred to Level 2 support and the status is changed to 'Transferred'.
- Once the Level 2 technician sees the incident in their queue, they change the status to 'Acknowledged' so that the Service Desk knows that the technician has acknowledged receipt of the incident.
- When the technician begins to work on this incident, the status is changed to 'Work In Progress'.
- If the technician is awaiting end-user response with additional information, the status can be changed to 'On-Hold' or 'Waiting on Customer'.
- If the technician needs to conduct further research to resolve the incident, then the status is changed to 'Researching'.
- Once the incident is resolved, the status is changed to 'Closed'.

By providing this level of granularity, the end-user can be constantly kept up-to-date on the exact status of their incident. Not having this capability would be (in our urban transport analogy) the equivalent of not providing commuters with detailed timetable information.

The Service Desk should also provide the capability to help determine customer education and training requirements. Always remember that the Service Desk is a single point of contact for end-users, and it is critical that capabilities exist to capture training or education requirements regarding a specific application or IT service. By incorporating this sort of capability, IT managers are transforming the Service Desk function from a reactive to a proactive model. Here, for example, the information could be used to provide line-of-business managers with the information they need to help develop training plans for new or existing end-users. This has a flow-on effect of reducing end-user downtime and driving higher productivity.

3.4 Choosing the Right Service Desk Model

There are several options for structuring the Service Desk function within an organization, and it is important that supporting technologies have the flexibility to support each of those models. Remember, a current Service Desk structure will not necessarily be the same in five or even perhaps within a single year's time, so look for solutions that can grow and change with the business needs. Common approaches for the Service Desk structure include:

- **The Local Service Desk** - provides optimal support for a single location. It is where the first level support is provided and the additional levels of support are localized for managing one location, and logging all calls into their own instance of the Service Desk application with no insight into other locations. For an organization with multiple locations, this means that each location will have its own Service Desk unit. To ensure that local Service Desks are effective for an IT organization with multiple business locations, you have to co-ordinate and maintain standardization across all of the local Service Desks. Centralized management reporting is often difficult due to manual consolidation and compiling of reports across the multiple Service Desks. For an IT organization that wants consistent management and reporting across the business regardless of location, the Local Service Desk structure is not the best option, and other models should be considered.

- **The Central Service Desk** - is preferred where all of the calls (irrespective of origin and location) are centrally logged. For IT organizations with multiple locations, this reduces operational costs and provides consolidated management reporting and performance statistics. It can leverage available resources across the business regardless of geographical location. It can consolidate Level 2 and higher support, so that all calls are managed at the centralized location.

- **The Virtual Service Desk** - incorporates the best of both worlds. The Virtual Service Desk is location agnostic. Due to technological advances, as long as there is connectivity between locations, having a Virtual Service Desk may be the optimum solution for your IT organization. This structure helps consolidate the tracking of the calls, yet, can distribute the first, second and third level of call management to the location of the call if necessary. This means that a single instance of an application would exist for consistency in managing the processes, statistics, escalations and notifications to manage the incidents, problems, changes and service requests; however, the support for the end-user can be provided by any support location. One caveat to this type of structure is that there needs to be one common language that is used in the Virtual Service Desk for data entry. This will become critical so that all resources across the globe can search on a common set of Known Errors, incident matching and problem diagnosis functions. The Virtual Service Desk is the most used of the Service Desk structures, providing a common language, common processes, procedures and common statistics, to cut costs, improve quality of services and increase customer satisfaction.

There are many other considerations that need to be considered when setting up a Service Desk. What are your business objectives for the Service Desk? What are the maturity levels of the IT organization that supports the business and what are the maturity levels of the business? What are the service expectations of the business? What are your organizations Key Performance Indicators (KPIs) to ascertain continual process improvements? Determining exactly what IT services you will be providing to the business is critical to success. Also important is the creation and publication of guidelines that document the levels of expected support that the Service Desk will provide to the business, so that both IT and the business understand what to expect from the Service Desk and related entities. If there is no initial data available on the levels of support being currently delivered, data should be accumulated for a minimum of two months before communicating what support levels can actually be expected at the present time. Examples of SLAs include establishing response times for specified types of calls, defining service priorities based on business impact and setting the time period before escalation. Always remember that careful planning will go a long way to avoiding problems further down the track. Even the best Service Desk function will be useless if the process it supports is deficient, or worse, just plain broken (you will simply be automating a broken process). So be sure to supplement technology with practical and outcome based assessment services that quickly gauge maturity levels and recommend service improvement strategies.

3.5 Further Optimizing the ITIL Service Desk Function

As the central hub or integration point between the Incident, Problem, Change and Configuration Management process tracks, and by leveraging Knowledge Management, the Service Desk is able to optimize the support services it provides to the business. As shown in figure 3.1, the Service Desk is the central point of contact between IT and the business. The Service Support Subway Map (figure 3.2) can be used to view all of the process lines, process activities (stations) and process intersections that occur along the P-D-C-A continuous quality improvement cycle, and how they relate to, and can be supported by the Service Desk function.

To ensure that the Service Desk is running at peak performance, it is also important to ensure that statistics are continuously collected, analyzed and acted upon. With the ability to track the types or categories of incidents and resolution times, it becomes easier to pre-determine where service improvements are required. Ensuring access to all of the data for accurate

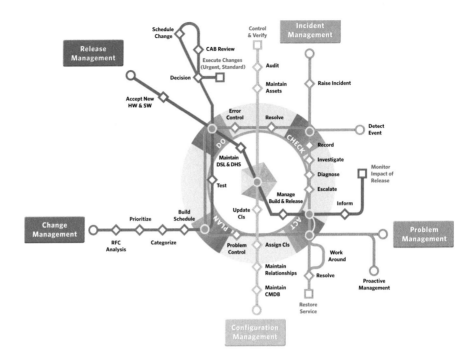

Figure 3.2 Service Support Subway Map

reporting will be critical, which is why an integrated capability is so important. However, data alone is not enough, and processes must be in place and automated to ensure that data is constantly measured and most importantly, used. The ability to integrate and measure across processes (ie Incident, Problems and Change Management) enables the organization to drive improvements. For example, providing visibility as to what % increase of problems result from RFC enables management to drive necessary process improvements in the Change Management process.

3.6 Selecting the Right Service Desk Application

Premier Service Desk applications:

- facilitate trending information across the support processes
- provide a vehicle to report KPIs on Service Desk activities such as:

    - total number of calls to the Service Desk
    - average call handling times by the Service Desk by category
    - % of total incidents resolved by the Service Desk

- % increase month over month of Closed on First Contact by the Service Desk
- % of Incidents caused by Changes in the Environment – Planned and Unplanned
- % increase of calls closed with associated knowledge documents (this will show that the knowledge created by Level's 2 and 3 are being done properly)

- provide integration between the Incident Management tracking and the Knowledge Management systems
- provide integration between the Problem Management tracking system and the known error database that is usually included in the Service Desk or the Knowledge Management system
- supply the ability to link incidents with problems with changes through automated workflow templates
- supply the ability to manage the work effort of calls within the system
- manage the status' of calls along with the proper categorization structure, and the prioritization, escalation and notification rules to ensure the proper level of service support to the business.

3.7 Avoiding Service Desk Problems

- **Communication is the key to success** – everyone involved in the Service Desk function must understand the processes that it directly manages and the interdependencies and relationships with other processes and procedures that it facilitates. The processes must be followed and information tracked effectively in the Service Desk application, so that everyone involved in the process knows the status of the call, who is performing what task, what has been done before them and the assigned period prior to escalation.

- **Track every single call that comes into the Service Desk** – and make sure that all calls are recorded and categorized properly. This will improve process management, the effectiveness of the Service Desk function and increased customer satisfaction.

- **Arm the Service Desk Function -** with the tools necessary to get their job done effectively. Make sure that there is an integrated capability that allows the tracking of RFCs, service requests, incidents and problems, so the business has a single contact point with IT.

Planning for and implementing a Service Desk function is one of the most critical components of a Service Support process improvement program. As stated at the beginning of this chapter, the Service Desk function is as vital as the information you might expect if you are an urban transit traveller; it facilitates your journey and exists to improve your experience.

You must initially determine the scope and structure of the Service Desk as well as understand what the focus of the Service Desk will be. You must also determine the type of Service Desk you will implement and how it will interface, not only with the end-user community, but also with the internal IT organization which is critical to the success of the Service Desk.

It is critical to understand the need to automate as many activities as possible, whilst leveraging the knowledge to support the Service Desk function, for mapping Known Errors and other knowledge in the environment. But remember, if you have broken processes or no processes at all, throwing a tool at it only serves to automate a broken process, so be diligent in your efforts.

You should establish the KPIs that the Service Desk will monitor and manage, to determine whether continual process improvements exist or, if processes change, that the changes made are going to be instrumental to the overall success of the Service Desk and increased customer satisfaction.

4 Incident Management

The objective of the Incident Management process is to return business to a normal service level, as defined in an SLA, as quickly as possible, with minimum disruption to the business. Incident Management should also keep a record of incidents for reporting, and integrate with other processes to drive continuous improvement. ITIL places great emphasis on the timely recording, classification, diagnosis, escalation and resolution of incidents. Within Incident Management the Service Desk plays a key function, acting as the first line of support and actively routing incidents to specialists and SMEs. To be fully effective, the Service Desk has to work in unison with other supporting processes. For example, if a number of incidents are recorded at the same time, the Service Desk analyst needs sufficient information to prioritize each incident. Technology can be a key contributing factor by ranking incidents according to business impact and urgency. Today, many tools enable the automatic recording of incidents within the Service Desk function, but lack the capabilities to correlate incidents and to associate them with business service levels.

In reviewing the Incident Management process journey (figure 4.1), it is necessary to assess each critical process activity (or station), and examine how technology can be applied to optimize every stage of the journey, ensuring arrival at the process terminus - the efficient restoration of IT services.

EVENT

Incident Management starts with an event that, according to ITIL, is not part of the standard operation of a service, and which causes or may cause, an interruption or reduction in service quality. Incidents can include hardware and software errors, and user service requests which are typically not associated with IT infrastructure failures (such as functional questions or requests for information, or requests to have user passwords reset).

DETECT

The first activity along the Incident Management process journey is the mechanism to detect incidents as they occur within the operational infrastructure, resulting in deviations from normal service. Users of IT

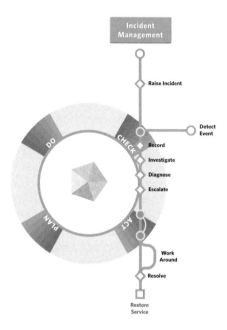

Figure 4.1 Incident Management Process Line

services are the first to detect service deviations, yet with automated management, IT can rapidly detect incidents before they adversely affect end-users and IT services. In some cases, IT can use process automation tools to detect errors before they affect IT service levels and to solve problems quickly before they impact the business.

In most cases incidents will be recorded by a Service Desk function. This should record all incidents to ensure that compliance with SLAs can be reported correctly. The location of an incident will determine who or what reports it. Naturally, users should have a facility to rapidly report incidents, supplying all information to the front line analyst, but a truly effective reporting function should also enable the system itself to record incidents automatically as they occur.

Many Service Desk solutions provide self-help and knowledge based capability, but even if users resolve the issue themselves, they should record the incident. This is important, since the IT function can proactively use an accurate base of recorded incidents to facilitate effective process improvements along other IT Service Management process lines. Also, giving end users the ability to log non-time critical incidents through a web enabled interface combined with a knowledge management tool, greatly reduces the number of calls made to the Service Desk.

Part of the Incident Management recording function should involve effective classification (to determine incident category) and matching (to determine whether a similar incident has occurred previously). Technology can help by providing front line support with information pertaining to the configuration items (CI's) supporting the end user who recorded the incident. During this phase Service Desk analysts review previous incident activity to understand the reason for the incident. The analyst should also have the means to classify the incident correctly using agreed coding criteria, identifying type of incident (eg IT Service=degraded) and the Service or CI affected (eg Order Entry Service). Many organizations mistakenly combine the IT Service/CI into the incident type. By doing so, they find that their incident classification methodology becomes far too complicated and people resort to classifying incidents incorrectly.

After classification, it is important to prioritize the incident properly. Service Desk solutions can help by automatically determining the priority based on the types of incident (eg IT Service=Outage), and the business services that are affected. The priority may also be determined by existing SLAs. After classification, the analyst should use incident matching to see whether a similar incident has occurred previously, and whether there is a solution, workaround or known error. If there is, then the investigation and diagnosis stages may be bypassed, and resolution and recovery procedures initiated.

If the incident has high priority and cannot be resolved immediately, the incident manager should create a linked problem record and initiate Problem Management process activities. Interestingly enough, Problem Management will have a different focus to Incident Management, and the two could be in conflict. Incident Management should restore the IT service while Problem Management should determine a root cause and update the status to a known error. In the majority of cases where there is a conflict, Incident Management should take priority, since it is more critical to restore normal service levels, even with workarounds.

Before continuing along our Incident Management process journey, it is worth considering how the effective detection, recording and classification of incidents (achieved thus far) can facilitate an 'optimum' journey along other ITIL process lines. In figure 4.2 we can see that after the detection and recording activities, the Incident Management process arrives at a critical point — the Check junction. Incident Management outputs derived from the timely detection and accurate reporting of incidents provide the means to be more proactive and optimize the Problem Management process. For example, the accurate recording of all incidents will assist Problem Management with the rapid identification of underlying errors.

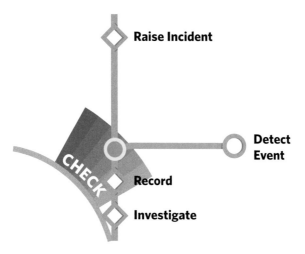

Figure 4.2 The CHECK Junction

Where justified, Problem Management will strive to correct these errors permanently, and reduce the amount of repeat incidents. Alternatively, the Check junction enables Incident Management to take inputs from Problem Management to further streamline the overall process. For example, by delivering information about known errors (from an integrated known error database) the 'journey time' to the ultimate destination - service restoration - will be reduced dramatically. Naturally, technologies can play a key role, integrating both Incident and Problem Management within a single solution.

If no immediate solutions are available, then the Service Desk function needs to be able to route incidents to SMEs. During the investigation and diagnosis phase, support analysts will collect updated incident details and analyze all related information (especially configuration details from a CMDB linked to the Service Desk).

During this phase, the support staff must have access to comprehensive historical incident, problem and knowledge data, centralized and maintained within the Service Desk. Also critical is the capability to augment incident management records with diagnostic data supplied by SMEs or via integrated management technologies. Management technologies can play a key role here in correctly identifying and routing incidents to the appropriate SMEs. By its very nature, investigation and diagnosis of incidents is an iterative process, and may involve multiple Level 1, 2 and 3 SME groups as well as external vendors. This demands discipline and a rigorous approach to maintaining records, actions, workarounds and corresponding results. Integrated Service Desk technology can help in this process by providing:

- flexible routing of Incident Management data according to geographic region, time, etc.
- automatic linkage and extraction of CMDB data for the examination of failed items
- a strong knowledge base and tools to expedite the diagnostic function
- management dashboards and reports to provide an overall status of Incident Management
- controls to ensure process conformance and provide comprehensive audit logs

Having conducted investigation and diagnosis, the Incident Management journey arrives at another station — Escalation. Critical here is the ability to escalate incidents rapidly, according to agreed service levels, and to allocate more support services if necessary. Escalation can follow two paths: horizontal (functional) or vertical. Horizontal escalation is required when the incident needs to be escalated to different SME groups who are better able to perform the Incident Management function. If not closely monitored, horizontal escalation can lead to incidents bouncing around the system without anyone taking ownership, with the increased likelihood of breeching SLAs. This is why it is so important to have a proactive approach and use process automation to route incidents correctly to the appropriate SME groups. Vertical escalation is where the incident needs to gain higher levels of priority. As part of the activity, it is essential that rules are clearly in place to ensure timely escalation, and avoid the need for support analysts to decide when to escalate - a recipe for disaster!

For every resolution attempt, accurate data must be attached to the incident detail to save repeating recovery procedures and lengthening overall resolution times. Technology can play another key role, automating the escalation process itself, and pinpointing the exact source of errors. This latter capability is important since it ensures the correct incident hand-off to appropriate SME groups early in the support cycle.

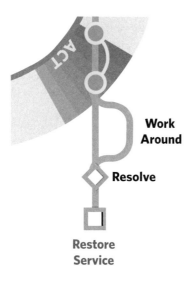

Figure 4.3 The ACT Junction

At this stage of the journey, the Incident Management process line has arrived at the ACT junction (see figure 4.3). Here, iterative investigation and diagnosis will have determined the nature of the incident, and what actions need to be initiated to resolve the problem. Customer service must be restored as quickly as possible (through workarounds if necessary), and incidents should be escalated to Problem Management in order to detect the underlying cause of the problem, provide resolutions and prevent incidents from reoccurring.

The final stage along the Incident Management journey is Resolution and Recovery. Here the main activities include resolving the incident with solutions or workarounds obtained from previous activities. For some solutions, an RFC will need to be submitted, so it is vital that technologies support the timely and accurate transference of incident details to a Change Management process. Once the solution is resolved by the SME groups, the incident is routed back to the Service Desk function, which confirms with the initiator of the incident that the error has been rectified and that the incident can be closed. During this phase, integrated technologies must support a number of service improvement functions, such as providing restricted access to the incident closing function, and ensuring that incidents are matched to known errors or problem records.

4.1 Optimizing the Incident Management Journey

Since a primary role of the Incident Management process is to ensure that users can get back to work as quickly as possible, activities should incorporate technologies that support the functions of recording, classification, routing to specialists, monitoring and resolution. As a minimum, tools that help enhance the Incident Management process should provide:

- facilities to automate the detection, recording, tracking and monitoring of incidents
- capabilities to ensure the integration of an accurate CMDB that will help estimate the impact of incidents according to business priority; integrated CMDB information also ensures that the support analyst has access to accurate information during critical diagnosis and investigation phases of the Incident Management process
- a comprehensive Knowledge Base (available to both users and support analysts) detailing how to recognize incidents, together with what solutions and workarounds are available
- strong workflow capability to streamline escalation procedures and ensure timely incident hand-offs between various support groups
- tight integration and proactive controls between supporting processes; for example, automatic logging of incidents during unapproved changes to configuration records
- total number of incidents
- average incident resolution time (by customer and priority)
- incidents resolved with agreed service levels (by customer and priority)
- incidents resolved by front-line support or through access to the knowledge base (with escalation and routing to SMEs)
- breakdown of incidents by classification, department, business service, etc.
- number of incidents resolved by analyst group/individual analyst/SME group, etc.

4.2 Potential Issues with Incident Management

The following is a list of issues to look out for to avoid problems in the Incident Management process:

- **Incident Management Bypass.** If users attempt to resolve incidents themselves, IT cannot gauge service levels and the number of errors. Technology can help by centralizing the Service Desk function — essentially acting as the clearing house for all incidents, and integrating Incident Management within a broader Incident, Problem, Change and Configuration Management process. Incident Management bypass can also happen by informally approaching the SME groups for help. From a process perspective, however, the SME group should not take on the work until the incident has been logged by the Service Desk function.

- **Holding on to Incidents.** Some organizations mistakenly fuse Information Management and Problem Management into a hybrid Incident Management process. This is detrimental from the perspective of metrics and the ability to prioritize the problems properly. There should be a clear separation between the two processes, and incidents should be closed once the customer confirms that the error condition has gone away. Based on business rules, the analyst can make the decision as to whether a related problem record should be created to look for a permanent solution.
- **Traffic Overload.** This occurs when there are an unexpected number of incidents. This may result in the incorrect recording of incidents leading to lengthier resolution times and degradation of overall service. Technology can help, by automating procedures to deploy spare capacity and resources.
- **Too many choices.** There is a temptation to classify incidents in finite detail and to make the analyst navigate through many sub-levels to select the incident type. This increases the time it takes to create the incident and will often lead to the incorrect classification, as the analyst gives up searching for the most appropriate match.
- **Lack of a Service Catalog.** If IT services are not clearly defined, it becomes difficult to refuse to provide help. A Service Catalog can help by clearly defining IT services, the configuration components that support the service, together with agreed service levels.

The objective of Incident Management is to restore services rapidly, in support of SLAs. Unlike Problem Management, whose focus is on finding the root-cause of problems, Incident Management is essentially about getting things back up quickly, even if this means performing workarounds and quick fixes.

Technologies can play a critical role in optimizing this process, by automating the actual process activities themselves (such as incident recording and classification), and by accessing the outputs from other related processes. Integration with other processes (for example Problem, Change, Configuration and Service Level Management) is especially important to ensure that incidents are kept to a minimum and that the highest levels of availability and service are maintained.

CHAPTER 5 Problem Management

The objective of the Problem Management process is to find the root cause of problems and to initiate actions to improve or correct the situation. The major activities within Problem Management include:

- **Problem Control** - for identifying problems and investigating their causes
- **Error Control** - for monitoring known errors through to successful resolution
- **Proactive Problem Management** – for identifying and eliminating problems before incidents occur
- **Providing Support Information** - for delivering problem information to other process areas and to IT management

Notably, Problem Management differs from Incident Management, which is focused on restoring service as quickly as possible. But many organizations struggle to control these distinct processes because they mistakenly try to combine them. One challenge is that the investigation of a problem's root cause may require periods of unplanned downtime, which Incident Management tries to avoid. By separating the two processes, responsibilities become clearer and the IT organization becomes more efficient.

Although the goals of Incident and Problem Management differ, the processes have a strong relationship. Problem Management supports the Incident Management process by providing workarounds and quick fixes. Incident Management supports Problem Management by providing comprehensive incident records to facilitate problem identification.

Problem Management includes both reactive and proactive activities. Reactive Problem Management aims to identify the root causes of incidents and present proposals for resolution by submitting RFCs. Proactive Problem Management aims to prevent incidents by working to identify weaknesses in the infrastructure and to correct them before they cause service disruption. Many IT organizations spend too much time in reactionary day-to-day problem resolution. Business value increases when IT becomes more proactive, providing problem-free IT services through preventative measures and controls.

Within Problem Management, several roles are needed to ensure that the process is functioning effectively. The Problem Process owner is responsible for determining the structure of the Problem Management team, as well as the tasks within the Problem Management process. The Problem Manager is responsible for managing the process while providing the mechanism

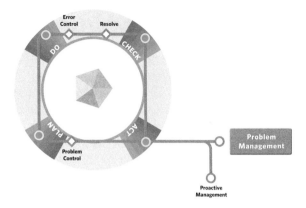

Figure 5.1 Problem Management Process Line

for proper execution. The Problem Manager also works with the Incident Manager to determine the criteria by which a single incident warrants the opening of a problem. Also, and based on previously agreed criteria, certain authorized staff within the Incident Management team can determine if a problem actually exists, and, if so, can involve the problem team to perform root-cause analysis while the Incident team concentrates on restoring the Service.

Before examining the Problem Management process in detail, it is important to review critical process integration points. By examining figure 5.1, we see that the Problem Management process line crosses each of the Plan, Do, Check and Act junction points of the continuous improvement cycle. During problem diagnosis, the process integrates with Incident Management (at the Act junction) to provide information about known errors, workarounds, and quick fixes, so that services can be restored faster and with minimal disruption. When known errors have been identified, Problem Management must integrate with Change Management (at the Plan and Do junctions) to ensure that RFCs are raised and implemented to resolve the problems. Once the change has been implemented, Problem Management again integrates with Incident Management (at the Check junction) to gather and analyze incident data to proactively identify problems.

Problem Management starts with Problem Control, which is responsible for identifying problems, investigating the root cause and the configuration items that are at fault. Problem Control also provides the Service Desk function and Incident Management with information and advice on workarounds. The goal of Problem Control is to advance problems to become known errors by diagnosing the unknown underlying root cause of the problem.

The first phase of Problem Control is to identify and record the problem. Problems can occur when events captured by incident management have an unknown root cause. In general, any incident with an unknown cause should be associated with a problem, but this practice is only worthwhile if there is a serious incident, or if the incident occurs repeatedly.

During this phase, information from Incident Management and from other processes is gathered by the Problem Management team for analysis. Strong process linkages must be in place to ensure that problem instances can be identified quickly.

Based upon the information gathered during the analysis phase, the Problem Management team will begin to determine the problem's root cause. To be successful, any Problem Management system must have the capability to link all associated incidents and configuration items (CIs) from the CMDB to the problem. Here, it may be necessary to create a parent problem with subsequent associated problems, so as to break up the multitude of potential problem areas for proper analysis and tracking.

Ensuring that single or multiple incidents can be linked to the problem, and that problems are linked to other associated problems, is critical for an effective Problem Management process. At the same time, the process must integrate with Change Management by initiating RFCs to address any known errors that have been identified.

After incident data has been collected for analysis, and a problem has been determined, it must be properly classified according to the category, impact, urgency, priority and status. Problem category identifies the problem area (for example, hardware or software) and all the CIs that affect the problem. Classification is accompanied by impact analysis on IT services (via the CMDB) to determine the seriousness of the problem, and the extent to which deferral of a solution is acceptable (urgency). Impact, urgency and business risk help determine the priority of the problem, as with Incident Management.

After the problem has been classified, the Problem Management journey begins an iterative process of problem investigation and diagnosis. As illustrated in figure 5.1, the Problem Management process line may be traveled several times before the root cause can be determined. During this phase, rapid response teams may meet to investigate and diagnose jointly the root cause of severe problems. Technology plays a critical role in this activity, helping pinpoint root cause across the technology domains that support IT services, such as Web services, applications, databases, servers and networks.

During the investigation and diagnosis phase, it is especially critical to have access to data on the status and the attributes of associated CIs (for example, access to information such as operating system level and security patches). Combined with the number and type of incidents and problems associated with the CI, this information can enable the Problem Management team to determine root causes and initiate error control activities more quickly.

If no immediate workaround or known error is available, then the Problem Management team continues to gather additional information for further diagnosis. Effective diagnosis of the underlying cause of the problem requires access to CI attributes (as discussed above) as well as any documentation or troubleshooting information from the Incident Management team. The Incident and the Problem Management system should be integrated to make this process seamless.

Throughout the Problem Management Process, other groups outside of the Problem Management team, such as application support, may be brought in to assist with problem diagnosis. In such cases, however, care must be taken to ensure that such teams work collaboratively to resolve problems, avoiding the more traditional and inefficient practices of attempting to resolve problems 'silo by silo'. Here again, advanced analytic and diagnostic tools can help to pinpoint the problem to a specific area and avoid unnecessary and time-consuming problem investigation.

If no immediate solutions are available it may be necessary to escalate the problem. Escalation schemes are essential to successful problem management. When Problem Managers meet with Incident Managers, escalated problems must be evaluated not only to expedite their resolution, but also to indicate potential future impacts to the business. Escalation schemes should also allow for the fact that classification of a given problem may change during its lifecycle (for example, when a seemingly minor problem becomes more critical after additional incidents are reported).

Once the cause of a problem and associated CI has been identified, it is assigned the status of known error and the Error Control activity begins. Error Control monitors known errors until they are resolved. This is achieved by raising RFCs to the Change Management process and by evaluating the effectiveness of changes in a Post Implementation Review.

During this phase, developing a known error database in accordance with knowledge management principles is critical to ensuring efficient and effective Incident Management and Service Desk functionality. The Service Desk function co-ordinates Incident and Problem Management activities and must leverage information contained within a Knowledge Database, which catalogs known errors and workarounds. Therefore, a knowledge tool is necessary that allows for flexible creation of known error records and ensures data accuracy and consistency. Known Errors shall not be placed in the Knowledge tool until Problem Management has analyzed and tested the work around and thus given authorization for their entry.

Other mechanisms can also save time and money during error control. For example, once a known error or workaround has been used to resolve an incident, the incident should be automatically linked back to the problem associated with the known error or workaround. This ensures that Problem Management teams can immediately see the effectiveness of workarounds and quick fixes. If an RFC has been issued and completed, a Post Implementation Review (PIR) needs to be initiated to ensure that everything went as planned and that the problem was truly resolved. Prior to actually initiating an RFC, the duration of the resolution process must be determined, together with the anticipated costs, and the cost/benefit to the business. If the business benefit is minimal, but the cost is high, then the resolution may be documented but not actually initiated.

PROACTIVE PROBLEM MANAGEMENT

The other aspect of Problem Management is Proactive Problem Management. While Proactive Problem Management takes a similar route to the 'reactive' journey discussed above, it aims to prevent incidents by identifying weaknesses and creating proposals to eliminate them. To build proactive capability, the Problem Management team can examine the incident repository and, via analysis of both current and past incidents, determine if there is a problem in the environment and then group these incidents into one problem.

Technology can support the Problem Management process by determining whether there are relationships between incidents and then automatically creating a problem. Obviously, such tools need strong analytical capability to determine trends and then create problems and link the evidence (incidents).

Proactive Problem Management also uses trend analysis to identify potential problems, and analyze situations where a CI under investigation could cause a failure elsewhere in the infrastructure. It should also allow better protection of IT services when failures have occurred in other areas. These benefits can be more effectively realized when data from a knowledge management tool facilitates faster associations, matching and resolution.

Integrated knowledge management tools enable the automatic population of attributes into an incident when a known error is associated with that incident. This will provide a greater level of accuracy to metrics by ensuring consistency. One example is the proper classification of the category for the incident, which may have been originally misdiagnosed. Another example is automatically linking the incident back to the original problem to keep gathering evidence and to allow greater visibility of the impact.

5.1 Optimizing the Problem Management Journey

Problem Management becomes truly optimized when integrated with other processes, such as Incident, Change and Configuration Management and incorporating Knowledge Management. The close relationships between these processes are represented visually in the process map (see Service Support Subway Map). Some of the support processes cross each other at different intersections, or junctions. This indicates a relationship between those processes where the outputs from one become the inputs to another.

As an example, Problem Management must gather data from Configuration Management including essential information about the infrastructure, such as CI status and change history. The CI information is an input to the Incident, Problem and Change process while the output to Configuration Management includes how many incident records were logged against a CI, or from Problem Management what known errors are linked to it. Armed with this information, Problem Management can raise an RFC to remove the problem from the environment, thus providing for fewer recurring incidents against the relevant CIs. Working together, the integration of Problem Management with other processes allows for faster and more efficient customer service and better control of the IT infrastructure.

5.2 Selecting the Appropriate Technology Solution for Problem Management

The primary role of the Problem Management process is to minimize the adverse impact of incidents and problems on the business caused by errors within the IT Infrastructure, and to prevent recurrence of incidents related to these errors. Tools that help enhance the Problem Management process should provide:

- facilitation of trending information for more proactive Problem Management
- capability to view CMDB attributes of both the discovered and static attributes to assist in the problem resolution process
- mechanisms to report KPIs on the Problem Management process; at a minimum, reports and service dashboards should be capable of proving the following:
  - total number of problems
  - average problem resolution time (and by priority)
  - number of incidents resolved by problems
  - % of problems resulting in an RFC.
  - % of the RFCs based on problems that had to be backed out
  - known error effectiveness (number of incidents tied to known errors)
  - number of problems as a direct result of failed or unapproved changes
  - number of workarounds created and known errors created
  - number of problems resolved by analyst group/individual analyst, etc.

5.3 Avoiding Problems and Issues

- **Communication is Key to Success.**Everyone involved in the Problem Management process must understand the importance of their role in the entire process. Ensuring that each team member understands the proper handling of information regarding associated incidents, problems, changes and CI information is critical to understanding the impact of that problem. Also, effective communication allows each role to know the status and progress of a given problem. It is also important that information is communicated back to the affected end users and management regarding these problems.
- **Effective known error creation**. The Problem Management team must understand what data is necessary for effective known error creation, categorization and workflow. Having a standard for required data types within the known error database is critical to performing effective management of information based on the known errors.
- **Having data available for trending.**Ensure that the information needed for trending analysis is tracked and available. A fully integrated toolset allows organizations to see information contained within the Incident Management solution and information on the Configuration Items, as well as access to the known error and knowledge database. Also important is a management dashboard illustrating what is happening in near real-time in the organization.

CHAPTER 6 Change Management

Change is an intrinsic aspect of every business - especially healthy businesses that innovate and readily adapt to shifts in the market. So, for a business to remain healthy, its IT organization must be capable of effectively and efficiently handling change. It must be able to execute change with minimal cost and minimal risk of business disruption. IT must also be able to keep itself well-aligned with changing business goals and priorities.

In today's fast-moving markets, this ability to easily and appropriately handle change is even more important. That's why IT organizations need to implement and automate best practices for the entire end-to-end change management lifecycle, from 'planning' through 'doing'. Only IT organizations that embrace this kind of disciplined approach to change management will be able to deliver the operational agility essential for service excellence. If Incident and Problem Management represent the 'heart' of Service Support, then Change Management is the process to control the 'heart rate'. Optimized Change Management results in fewer incidents and problems, and helps ensure that strategic improvement requests are quickly processed and implemented. That is why the process must be well documented, especially during categorization activities, since decisions made here will affect how resources and costs will be allocated.

In reviewing the Change Management process journey (see figure 6.1), it is necessary to assess each critical process activity (or station), and to examine how technology can be applied to optimize every stage of the journey.

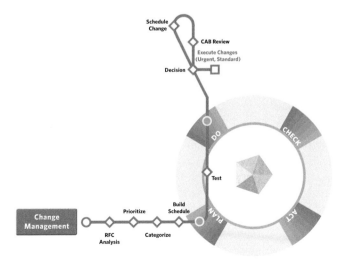

Figure 6.1 Change Management Process Line

While technology will greatly enable the automation of the change process, it cannot improve a process that is fundamentally poor.

The journey of Change Management starts with an RFC. What is the difference between a service request and a change? At a basic level, a service request may involve making a change to the environment, but generally that change is operational and does not impact business services. A number of related service requests could generate a change if they require impact analysis or touch the production environment.

An RFC could be triggered by such activities as a customer request via the Service Desk, the introduction or removal of a Configuration Item, or the output of a development project. It could also be triggered by Problem Management. To prevent too many entry points, the process should document who can create RFCs, what they are intended to do and what information is required.

Technology can help, ensuring that, requestors don't need to know the entire process and have a simple way of submitting RFCs. The tool should drive them through the important steps and ensure that the correct level of detail is captured. It is also important to understand the business importance of the change.

Remember, the goal of Change Management is to facilitate all change requests by using clear procedures, automation and easy checks and balances. ITIL suggests that any member of the organization should be able to submit an RFC. If not managed properly, this could lead to un-gated demand and possible misuse of the Change Management system. A more appropriate approach would be to use service requests for routine standardized demands that need not be controlled by Change Management, and to use IT or business relationship managers to submit RFCs.

RFC ANALYSIS

This activity of RFC Analysis is designed to perform an initial evaluation of the information provided for completeness and feasibility. An automated system can significantly shorten this phase by allowing the tool to apply business rules to determine what information is required. A key requirement is ensuring that adequate change lead times are in place, and in-line with policy.

After performing the initial analysis, the next station is prioritizing the change. This occurs by analyzing the impact of the problem and the urgency of the fix (if the change was generated from a problem) or the importance to the organization of what the change is implementing. If this cannot be agreed upon, the Change Advisory Board (CAB) may need to intervene. When the change priority is established it is used to determine resource requirements and change scheduling windows. In a resource-constrained environment, business units can use it to prioritize demand internally.

Risk assessment should also be determined at this stage. Measuring risk can be defined as the actual risk associated with implementing the change versus the risk of possible failures if changes are not implemented. Both types of risks should be evaluated and costed. Another portion of determining risk is based on the impact of the change on other components of the environment. Today, in a highly shared environment, an individual cannot track all of the touch points between technology and business services. For example, if a change requires a clustered web server to be rebooted, what business services are affected and what is the impact on SLAs? Integration with Configuration Management can help by allowing you to work through 'what if' scenarios to determine the impact of a technology change on business services.

CATEGORIZE

The next station is actually a major hub for a number of activities. Categorization involves evaluating the size of the change from a resource requirements perspective, the risk associated with the change, as well as the priority, and then deciding on the process steps to be followed. Categorization is an extremely important activity, since it is assigned according to business impact, and therefore determines the level of change authorizations and financial and resource requirements. During this stage, IT must collaborate with the business to ensure the correct categorization of changes and avoid problems further down the line.

The bulk of Change Management work is done at this station, with many checks and balances to ensure that change approval becomes relatively straightforward. Here, organizations can realize the major benefits of Change Management, for example, by utilizing technologies to help determine change categories (based on criteria agreed with the business), and to quickly absorb large volumes of changes and cost changes before they are incurred. For a minor change, a small number of workflow tasks should be completed and, for the most part, these will involve approvals and implementation scheduling. A minor change is appropriate only where a small amount of effort and risk is involved. Similar categorization can be used for significant changes. This is another area where technology can streamline and automate the process itself, using business rules to insert the correct process flow into the change and then to report conformance against the workflow whilst also providing an audit trail.

BUILD SCHEDULE

Once the RFC has been analyzed and categorized, the next stage includes building the schedule for provisioning hardware and software, and performing the work needed to put the change together. Decisions are made here such as what do we build and what do we buy in order to assess the financial impact. We will also consider any risks involved with the build and what the schedule for procurement of additional hardware or software might be.

TEST

The change needs to be tested in a pre-production environment to make sure that it is given every chance of success. Back-out plans and a 'go/no-go' decision point must be specified ahead of time. You do not want to leave such decisions in the hands of the implementers, as this encourages a 'hero' culture where people will keep trying to implement a change and make it work. This is a poor practice as it generally means that the change process did not work and there is a higher risk of the change failing or having undesirable impacts on its related IT services.

DECISION

Once this work has been performed, a decision is made on whether to proceed. This will happen at the Change Advisory Board (CAB) meeting. Minor changes should be authorized prior to the CAB meetings, which should focus on change requests that have higher risk and associated costs.

Again, this is why the business must be involved from the design phase of process development. Everyone needs to understand what is critical to the business to determine changes that can be pre-approved and those that need to be analyzed further.

CAB REVIEW

The CAB should consist of all the interested parties for active changes, both from IT and the business. The CAB should meet regularly and involve a formal meeting, including meeting minutes and communication. The CAB should review all proposed and implemented changes (this is the Post Implementation Review). For new changes, there should be agreement on the need, resource allocation and available funds. A lot of work is required after CAB approval, which is why it is important to automate what can be complex processes. The CAB should also review implemented changes to determine the quality of the process and whether the changes were implemented correctly. Determining that the technical aspect of the change was successfully implemented is insufficient. It is necessary to determine whether the change achieved its purpose.

More mature organizations will wait for a specified period before closing off the change. IT should demonstrate its engagement with the customer at the CAB stage by ensuring that business customers affected by changes are fully involved in the decision-making process. The CAB has responsibility for approving or rejecting changes. They also should perform the due diligence and, in instances where there is not enough information, make a decision to send the change back to the requester. Approval must be gained at three levels: technical, business and financial. Since these CAB meetings can require significant time and resources, technology can be effectively utilized, for example, by giving CAB members electronic access to RFCs for electronic approval.

Once the CAB reviews the change and has accepted the release package, the 'doing' phases of scheduling and implementation begin. The CAB has to be financially responsible and strike a balance between managing risk and controlling costs.

Once all approvals are given, it is now appropriate to schedule the change. More activities need to happen before a change window can be selected. In cases of major releases, an organization may be restricted to certain maintenance windows and needs to have a place holder in the FSC calendar. These key activities are best controlled by using best practice project management. This is one of the key steps in increasing the value and taking advantage of the proactive nature of Change Management.

Scheduling should be worked out with the key stakeholders to ensure that all the implementation steps required to institute the change are achievable. Automated technology helps keep everyone informed of what needs to be done and when it is needed.

Providing visibility into when changes are to be implemented is critical. In this scheduling phase, an FSC should be updated. This should be a generally available calendar view of when all change windows are scheduled. It should be clearly stated within each window whether any (business) services or technologies will be impacted, along with the start and end time of the implementation. This is important for a number of reasons. First, it allows changes to be implemented together where there is an opportunity to do so (for example where there is common infrastructure being affected). Secondly, it provides the ability quickly to spot change conflicts or situations where the time of the planned change could have a detrimental affect on the business (for example, if the business is running a sales campaign it would be inconvenient if certain Web services were unavailable during that time). And third, it makes the Service Desk aware of planned change and service outages so they can place an advance notice on the bulletin board and are prepared to answer the influx of calls. Otherwise, the Service Desk will waste time trying to diagnose the increase in incidents caused by the service outage or implemented change.

Only the changes that are approved and scheduled in the change window can be implemented. This is not an opportunity for people to introduce unauthorized changes. The entire premise of the Change Management process is to protect the production environment; unauthorized changes put this objective at risk. An output at this stage will be an implementation report that will be reviewed at the next CAB meeting to ensure that the business goals were met, and the risks and costs to the business were minimized.

Including the business in this process allows for continuous improvement because you are constantly engaged to ensure the change process is aligned with the business goals. If they are not, you may not meet the business objectives and be forced instead to refine your process to make the necessary changes. All the discussion above has been in the context of a well planned process where forewarning is imbedded into the change process. In a dynamic operational environment there will often be times when high-impact incidents and problems need to have fixes applied that will involve a change to the production environment. This is not an opportunity to bypass the change process as there should also be a process in place to handle urgent or emergency changes. Change approval is still a prerequisite in these cases, but the standard process will generally be condensed and some of the CAB approvals will be delegated.

Organizations that have not fully developed their Change Management processes will see a high volume of emergency changes, most likely because of timing. This is normally due to lead times not being enforced, with changes continuously and mistakenly viewed as emergencies. A good metric to gauge whether a change is an emergency is to determine if there is a high impact incident or problem open that this change will fix. If this is not the case, then you must question whether it is an emergency change.

The last step is to review the Change Management process as an entire unit. Change Management is an iterative process that requires constant review and adjustment for continuous improvement. This is why the process owner should constantly be reviewing changes to look for ways to make the process better and to consult with the business regularly, to ensure their needs are being met.

6.1 Ensuring a Successful Change Management Journey

In simple terms, the underlying goal of Change Management is to protect the business, because any time that we touch the production environment we put the business at risk. Failed changes are better than changes that are successfully implemented and cause failures later. But both are bad. It is not good enough just to have a good Change Management process. Compliance is also required to make sure things are done as they should be and that a full audit trail of everything that was done is easily accessible. To do this process manually in a complex environment is very difficult and prone to human errors or having people bypass the system.

To raise the level of maturity where business impact and risk assessment is performed requires integration with Configuration Management. Configuration Management will provide Change Management with a baseline, priority and urgency of changes, and detailed information on the history and relationships of Configuration Items. This is necessary in order to affect a complete impact assessment of changes made.

Integrated technology and process automation solutions can significantly ease the overhead of managing the process through automation and ensuring process compliance. Ways include:

- embed a change process in the solution based on the change category; analysts can then select the appropriate workflow template to assign individual tasks automatically to the appropriate resource in the change process

- assist the CAB by providing information to the relevant people electronically, so they do not actually need to come together to discuss changes unless there is a specific reason
- ensure conformance to the process by not allowing the change to progress unless the prerequisite tasks have been completed, and a record is made of who completed them and when
- perform business impact analysis through Configuration Management to determine what business services are impacted by changes to the infrastructure; often, without this link to Configuration Management, it is nearly impossible to determine all the impact points that a single change can cause, since there is no relationship information in the infrastructure
- unify change processes across both IT operations and software development
- allow the Change Management process to be a business enabler where the repeatable process is constantly used without the requestor having to try and work out what needs to be done
- Service Levels can be offered for Change Management and business rules can be used to proactively monitor these and raise visibility automatically when a violation occurs
- engage with the customers and make them part of the Change Management process, using facilities such as portfolio management to prioritize strategic change requests

CHAPTER 7 Configuration Management

The objective of the Configuration Management process, as defined by ITIL, is to provide a logical model of the infrastructure or a service by identifying, controlling, maintaining, verifying and reporting of configuration items in existence including their version, constituent components and relationships.

In other words, Configuration Management is the process in charge of the underlying referential that other processes use to enable or facilitate their activities. This infrastructure or service referential is usually called a CMDB, and contains all relevant details of identified and controlled resources of the IT infrastructure called Configuration Items (CI) and their relationships.

Configuration Management should be considered to improve performance, increase process maturity, help answer questions and empower decision-making. Indeed, everyone would agree the quality of a decision mainly depends on the quality and accuracy of the information you have at the time of the decision. How many times have you have made a decision without partial or vertical information? How many times have you lacked the information needed to support a critical decision-making process? For example, have you ever faced the following questions? Should I escalate this Incident? Is this Incident a direct cause of a Change? Should we accept this Change? Is this point the root cause of this Incident or just a side-effect? Will this Change impact or put the business at risk? How difficult it is for IT Financial Management to get information from Operations? How easy is it to link unavailable resources to service unavailability? How do I optimize software licenses and cost? We could write a full book of questions the IT organization has to answer everyday.

Of course, most of this information mentioned already exists in formal or informal databases, Excel spreadsheets or in people's minds. Unfortunately, these are islands of information and because they are disconnected, they cannot support critical decision-making.

Configuration Management (figure 7.1) is all about connecting the information islands to enable efficiency. The CMDB may then be considered as an IT portal (the pentagon). This is where tools and technology can significantly ease CMDB implementation and adoption.

All along the configuration management journey, it is critical to keep in mind: the CMDB federates information, but should not replace existing information systems which have special built-in functions.

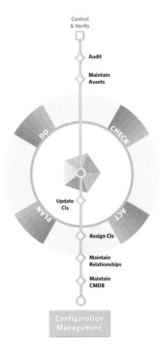

Figure 7.1 Configuration Management Subway Line

A common mistake is to visualize CMDB as an asset management extension. Configuration and Asset Management disciplines have different objectives and characteristics (figure 7.2).

	Configuration	Asset
Focus on	Business	Technical Infrastructure
Objectives	Enable Decisions	Inventory Technical Equipment
Resources Managed	Service, Hardware, Software, Document, Organisation, Security, Financial, Service Support, Procedure, Project...	Hardware and Software Information
Traces	Detailed	Limited
Attributes	Reduced to Strict Minimum	Very Detailed and Large
Relations	Logical, Extended and Flexible	Technical and Basic

Figure 7.2 Configuration vs. Asset

Each appears as a record in the CMDB, referring to an identified and controlled resource (figure 7.3).

An easy way to define a CI is to use the STAR model:

- **Status** - define the current state of the item and CI life cycle management
- **Traces** - contain item history, ie all modifications applied on this record such as record creation, status change, owner, etc.
- **Attributes** - characterize related resource such as name, serial number, memory, CPU, version number
- **Relations** - list valuable logical relations with other CIs such as 'is installed on', 'is based on', 'utilize', 'refer to', 'owned by'

Imagine a spider's web connecting configuration items (figure 7.4). This enables the Service Desk analyst to navigate from a natural starting point: the end-user profile; it enables the Change manager to run through hardware and services impacts from a changed application; the Service Level manager to look after SLA optimization via related CIs; the Contract manager to optimize costs by watching CIs' usage. According to ITIL documentation this web is called the CMDB Structure.

Now that the objectives and the structure of a CMDB are understood, it is possible to begin the journey on the configuration subway line.

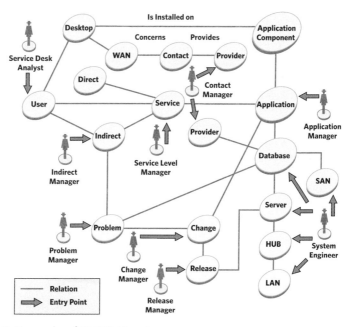

Figure 7.3 Example of CMDB Structure

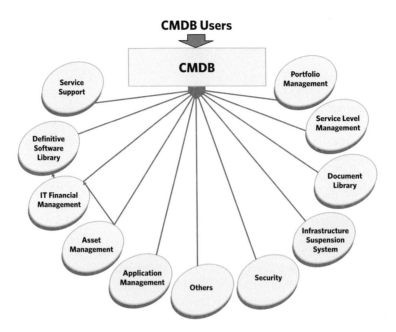

Figure 7.4 CMDB Federates IT Information

Plan

Each time you take a trip, you need to plan and define the purpose, scope, objectives, policies and procedures of your journey. In other words, define where you want to be once your CMDB is in place. To do so, you may want first to clearly define the users of your CMDB and their respective needs. A possible approach consists in collecting a list of questions. Those questions then help to line up expected benefits, estimating associated costs and evaluating critical success factors. As you understand the above, it is critical to have a clear vision of the actual situation. Implementing Configuration Management is everything, except simple. Keeping the momentum and your CMDB accurate is even more difficult. Therefore, it is extremely important to have - up-front - a clear and formal vision on the required human resources, with clear roles, responsibilities, procedures, rules, security policies, organization, and high-level structure and technical interfaces.

Your traveling companion on this ride should include Change Management. Since the level of information you gather will also be subject to sound Change Management approval, it is important to consider having them along for the ride. This prevents the creation of horizontal process silos.

Finally, it is vital to establish an adequate communication plan to make sure that internal and external partners are on board, and that someone is waiting at the destination to pick you up.

Identify

When your trip is planned, it is time to think about the things you want to bring with you. It is something which a lot of people dislike. In fact, it is always a challenge to find the right balance between having too much and not enough, or deciding what is useful or and what is unnecessary. Traveling with a lot of luggage can quickly become a nightmare. Arriving at your destination with a lack of luggage may cost you money.

In Configuration Management, you must identify and select the structure of your CMDB. You must agree on configuration item classes, the level of detail required for each, life cycles, naming conventions, possible relations, load strategy and reconciliation rules. If the item is to be classified as a true CI, it would be the lowest common denominator of independent change, or it would then be considered an attribute. It should also be relevant to a Service being provisioned.

Based on what you identify as required, you now need to select and set up the most appropriate 'luggage'. The challenge is to define when and where a CIs' life cycle begins and the right method to collect, load and initialize CIs in your CMDB. Two approaches are typically used:

- **Automated** - tools are set up to collect in real time or to batch information from sources
- **Manual** - processes and procedure are defined to ensure CMDBs accuracy and coherence

Most of the time, it would be a mixture of both. When automated, two methods can be considered (push and/or pull) and data must be segmented based on the level of accuracy. For example, the status must be as accurate as possible since it is one of the first decision criteria. Based on the level of detail, you may want to consider multiple load strategies (real time, every five minutes, every hour, half day, once day). Because data from different sources may be incoherent or redundant, naming convention and reconciliation rules should not be underestimated.

In this activity, the asset database is a key source of information and a very good starting point. Asset Management tools usually provide the mechanism to inventory technical information automatically.

MAINTAIN RELATIONSHIPS

The primary added-value of a CMDB is the ability to put a CI in the context of the Information system through its logical relationship with other CIs. This is done by bringing islands together. Unfortunately, this is not an obvious task. Even if most of the time, the information exists to a certain degree within the organization; the relationship is not necessarily obvious or formal. It may not even exist. Sometimes, sophisticated rules are required to convert a set of information into a formal logical relation. For example, to create a relationship between hardware equipment and contract, it might be necessary to compare hardware date of acquisition with contract life time. To identify services related to a server unit, it might be necessary to retrieve application transactions running on multiple application servers based on a central database installed on our server.

Establishing relationships should drive you to extend your source of information to application management databases, infrastructure supervision database, security database, network analysis system and others.

Once again, automated and manual approaches should be considered.

UPDATE CI's

When you travel in groups, you have two possible approaches in order to make sure that nothing is forgotten. You either nominate someone to be responsible for everything, or you assign responsibilities to individuals across the group; for example, everyone is responsible for their own belongings, someone is responsible for maps and someone else for tickets.

To ensure that the CI is actually properly managed, it must be owned by someone in the organization. This way, we can control and manage the risk of deviation between the view provided by the CMDB and the reality. It should be remembered that information collected should already be 'owned' by someone in the organization. Maintaining this ownership helps adoption and avoids redundant maintenance processes.

MAINTAIN CI's

With ticket (Configuration Plan) in your right hand, and luggage (CMDB) in the left hand, it is now time for departure. However, expect that unexpected events may happen.

The CMDB provides a view of a changing world. To match CIs with events happening in the information system, links with changes, incidents, problems and releases are required. When an incident occurs, the status of a CI might be affected. When a change is released on the infrastructure, a CI's status, attributes and relations might be affected. Therefore, at those times, automated or manual procedures should be defined to ensure efficient update of CIs. ITIL recommends that every change of attributes and relations should be updated with a related RFC to ensure the right parties are notified. Of course, the ownership plays an important role in this activity.

In case attributes are loaded from other sources, data must stay coherent. Usually, the change of the attribute happens in the source information system, which updates the CMDB via automated load processes. With hardware and software, automated inventory would detect changes and keep up-to-date the asset database and then the CMDB.

When a resource is removed from the IT infrastructure, the CI should to be decommissioned and archived. This is critical for 'trace-ability' and audit purposes. Some companies may view this point as vital if they have to comply with regulations such as SOX, Basel II, Solvency II, ISO/IEC 17799 or ISO/IEC 20000.

Another important consideration is the versioning of CIs. When creating a new version of a CI, information cleansing needs to be in place to ensure that only valuable information is retained along with active links. For example, information cleansing would remove links with closed calls, closed incidents, closed changes, closed releases, inactive relations to other CIs and traces (logs, history). Why do we have to consider this versioning functionality?

- The primary reason is flexibility. Indeed, along the life of a CI, the number of links may grow very quickly and dramatically. This growth will make CI records difficult to read; make configuration management into a real challenge; make audit even more complex; and impact CMDB performance and administration. Large organizations with millions of records in their CMDB have thousands of links added everyday.

- The second reason is functional. This feature is extremely useful in the management of resource versions. For example, in the case of the release of a new version of an application, three scenarios might be considered:
  - You change the version attribute of an Application CI Record. This is usually the case when you change an application located at one place in your infrastructure.
  - You create a new CI record for this new application. This is usually the case when you install a brand new version of an application in a new environment.
  - You version your CI record. This is usually the case when you upgrade an application on existing environments.

> **MAINTAIN ASSETS**

In terms of assets update and maintenance, even if the CMDB and the Asset database are obviously different they are also closely related. Based on where your CIs' life cycle starts, a CI may appear in your CMDB first. It will only appear in your asset database at the time the physical resource is installed in your infrastructure. Therefore synchronization policies, rules, procedures and mechanisms are required to ensure the global coherence of the information. We already underlined the need to update the CMDB when the asset database is updated; in some cases there is also a need to update or post-check the asset database when the CMDB is updated.

Two activities strongly recommended by ITIL best practices as a part of asset maintenance are:

- label physical resources and register labeled identifiers in your CI record in order to simplify asset localization; technologies such as bar coding, optical readers, localization ships could be used to ease the maintenance of assets and CIs

- control licenses to manage cost and the risk of noncompliance

Based on your organization, your company culture and the maturity of your Configuration Management process, it might be more efficient to manage label and licenses in your CMDB rather than your asset management system.

```
┌─────────────────────────────┐
│        ┌───────────┐        │
│        │   AUDIT   │        │
│        └───────────┘        │
└─────────────────────────────┘
```

Back to our trip, it is time for arrival at your destination. Before leaving the train, we should check that everything is in place.

Implementing a CMDB in an organization takes quite some time and requires a progressive approach to enable proper adoption and use. A CMDB which is not up-to-date and is essentially unusable will not be used. The purpose and expected benefits of, and investment in Configuration Management would then become obsolete.

To avoid that situation, the following audit activities are required:

- **Baseline -** establish a snapshot of your CMDB or a subset of your CMDB used to monitor the evolution of your system; it could also be used to refer back and rebuild a specific version at a later date
- **Configuration Control -** ensure that no CI is added, modified, replaced and removed without an approved change request to guarantee the reliability of your CMDB
- **Status Accounting -** enables tracking of the status as a CI changes from one state to another in order to control the coherence of the CMDB
- **Verification -** ensure the accuracy of your CMDB through a series of reviews and audits to verify the physical existence of the CI and the recording process of CIs

Those activities allow you to estimate CMDBs deviations. Because a deviation means a risk and nothing is perfect in this world, a deviation risk acceptance level should be defined upfront, to ensure awareness and re-enforce adoption.

7.1 Configuration Management — The Subway to Success

Experience has proven that the benefits that companies can expect from Configuration Management are huge in term of business alignment, performance optimization, quality of delivered services and cost management. But the challenge is at the level of the expected benefits. Configuration Management is complex because it requires rigorous processes, formal approach, appropriate communication plans and global adoption from the organization. The subway approach helps you to keep your Configuration Management process as simple as possible.

A lot of companies have made the mistake of underestimating the initial investment and by focusing on the tool before the process. Of course, the tool is critical to the success of a Configuration Management initiative. Fortunately, all the technologies required to implement, manage and integrate a CMDB have already existed in the market place for a number of years.

This is where tools and technology can significantly ease the overhead of managing the process, through automation and ensuring process compliance. This can help by:

- enabling integration with various sources of information
- enabling strong integration with change and release management
- enabling integration with other IT processes
- facilitating ease of implementation of other IT Service Processes
- enabling audit activities with the accurate reports, mechanism and navigation tools
- supporting baseline, versioning and reconciliation mechanisms
- providing graphical visualization of your CMDB structure to ease analysis
- supporting security strategy and access control
- implementing a quick and flexible approach
- understanding CMDB User requirements
- automating rules and procedures
- controlling and management of CI life cycles
- automating as much as possible to minimize bureaucratic activities
- developing a robust communication plan
- defining clear roles and responsibilities
- sharing information among the organization
- creating a single point of access through a centralized Information portal
- building awareness from the top down and across the organization

8 Configuration Management Database (CMDB) Function

Before ITIL® entered the scene, IT managers tended to look at IT as a collection of applications chosen to meet technical requirements. If a site had a problem with support, they looked for a better Service Desk. If ordering from IT was unreliable, they looked for a new Service Catalog. The need to meet requirements has not gone away, but ITIL has placed requirements in a new perspective. The ITIL framework prompted IT managers to look at IT *services* first and requirements second. The requirements are important, but now they are viewed as part of a larger more important initiative: to support and deliver efficient and cost-effective services to the business. As a result, it is no longer enough to meet the requirements from the IT groups that exist as silos. IT must fit together into one consistent practice that supports the needs of the business. Automation is driven by the needs for IT to deliver on the initiative. The transition from an IT department to one that delivers and supports business processes and their underlying IT services does not happen overnight. It is a journey. And when the journey appears to be over, it starts all over again in a continuous service improvement cycle.

A well managed IT organization optimizes business services by minimizing risks and maximizing return while achieving enterprise goals. These services and goals are not static. They change continually with changing circumstances and competition. To deal with the dynamic nature of business, the concept of continuous improvement has developed.

A CMDB and the Deming Cycle are two paradigms that lie at the foundation of continuous improvement of IT management and governance. The CMDB helps IT managers focus on business services as well as IT technology by providing a comprehensive view of the IT environment. Over time, IT departments that use these strategies tend to reduce and conquer the complexity that always threatens to overwhelm IT. The Deming Cycle (sometimes called the 'Shewhart Cycle') is a continuous quality improvement model that provides continuous feedback to guide organizations towards optimal strategies. When applied to IT, the cycle relies on the CMDB, and supports ITIL best practices.

The Deming Cycle is very simple (figure 8.1): **Plan** what you intend to do, then **Do** it. Study and **Check** the results, then **Act** on the study and begin the cycle again. More succinctly: Plan, Do, Check, and Act (P-D-C-A).

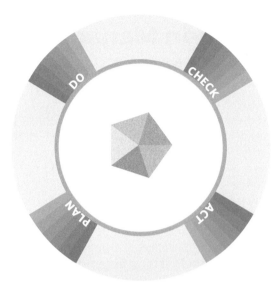

Figure 8.1 The Deming Cycle with the CMDB in the center

The Deming Cycle appears in many places. ITIL® relies upon it. Control Objectives for IT (COBIT®) is built around the Deming Cycle. Six Sigma® has very similar feedback cycles, as does the Software Engineering Institute Capability Maturity Model®. Whether the business is a service like printing, or an activity like installing a new LAN segment, the P-D-C-A cycle results in a basic pattern for service improvement.

An improvement methodology in a vacuum is not enough; a solid base of information is required. IT management and governance can be built on different data foundations, but one that fits the need best is a CMDB.

IT is buzzing about CMDBs, but what exactly is a CMDB? It is not a data store. The CMDB is an application that *uses* a data store, (which is usually a relational database), but the CMDB itself is not the database. Instead, it is a virtual representation of the real infrastructure configuration (what actually exists: people, processes and assets) as defined by the application and process which uses configuration data to guide IT operations. Without the Application and Configuration Management process, the data is inaccessible and quickly becomes stale and inaccurate. The principles for using and maintaining a CMDB come from the ITIL.

A CMDB contains the significant items in the IT infrastructure and the relationships between these items. The items are called CIs. A hardware asset, software and its licenses, a business service, a process, a document, a contract, a person and an organization can all be considered CIs in the IT infrastructure. The relationships between CIs that make up critical business services are also vital to a useful CMDB. 'Backs up', 'governs', 'documents' and 'links to' can all be CMDB relationships. The criterion that distinguishes CIs and CI relationships from an asset repository is their importance to the IT infrastructure and links to the vital business processes.

The CMDB has generated a set of specialized terminology:

- **Scope** is the choice of items in the infrastructure to be managed as CIs within the CMDB.
- **Depth** is the choice of attributes to associate with each CI in the CMDB.
- **Synchronization** is the way CMDB data is kept in alignment with the real infrastructure.
- **Federation** is a broad subject that addresses the way CI attributes, relationships, and application information are incorporated into a CMDB, from multiple sources.
- **Reconciliation** is the way federated data from many sources are tied together and correctly associated with a single CI.

There are several influential sources of guidance for CMDB policies including ITIL and ISO/IEC 20000. COBIT provides a more financially oriented view of IT management policies. Several industry leaders (eg BMC, CA, IBM, HP, and Fujitsu) have formed a working group for establishing a standard-based design for CMDB federation. However, each company ultimately chooses their own practices and policies for scope, depth and synchronization according to their Configuration Management process. For example, one business may choose to scope their CMDB down to a few accounting servers and factory floor controllers. A trading firm might include all their servers, network gear and even the traders' desktops. Some enterprises will find a sparse set of attributes adequate; others will go deeper with more attributes. It all depends upon the nature of a company's business and the services IT must deliver.

Companies also differ in their approach to control the accuracy of the CMDB. After initial population, their CMDB might be tightly governed by a CAB. Any change to the CMDB would have to come from an authorized change order, not from a discovered change in the real infrastructure. The CMDB should be periodically synchronized against the real infrastructure configuration, but this practice mandates that changes are made to the real infrastructure to match the CMDB, not the reverse. At these companies, the CMDB is normative; it represents the way the CIs are supposed to be configured, not the way they are configured, although everyone hopes the two will match.

At the other extreme, a company might eschew change control entirely and strive to keep the CMDB closely aligned with the real infrastructure. If governed by a CAB, changes to the CMDB would be representative of the real infrastructure – changes would be proactively controlled through

Change Management. Proponents of this approach argue that a CMDB containing data that is fully synchronized with the real devices is more useful for troubleshooting and analysis than normative data. Some feel that rigid change control is an obstacle to rapid evolution of the infrastructure. Both views have proponents.

8.1 CMDB and the Deming Cycle

The key to a successful journey lies where the routes intersect. There, the system must be managed carefully to work together smoothly and keep the journey on course. The CMDB is vital because all the process tracks meet in or around the CMDB. If it does not do its job, train wrecks are hard to avoid.

Plan

The Deming Cycle provides a good start for looking at the role of the CMDB. To see what the CMDB has to offer it is necessary to look at the cycle in some detail and at what a CMDB provides. The planning stage of any undertaking requires a master plan. Practitioners must be able to see what they have to work with, how the parts fit together and where opportunities present themselves. Without this knowledge, the planner is working by chance, laying plans that may fail because they do not correspond to the reality of the situation.

CMDB is the master blueprint for planning in the IT infrastructure. For example, suppose Acme Co. decides to consolidate two data centers. The CFO visits one data center and notices that it is almost completely vacant. A decision is quickly made to close the empty center and move all the remaining equipment to another site several hundred miles away; however, someone has to actually plan the move. The simplest plan is to shut everything down in the data center, throw everything on a truck, drive it to the new location, hook everything up and turn it back on.

Most system administrators will tell you this is a risky plan. Why? In IT, nothing ever appears as it seems. The significance of the equipment at one location is largely determined by the relationships and dependencies between the components. The dependent components may be widely distributed geographically and not easily identified.

An apparently insignificant server can be a link in a chain that supports critical business processes. Unfortunately, in a complex and ever changing environment, where both equipment and the people who administer it are in continuous flux, predicting the effects of a given change is very difficult.

Configuration Item List		Search	Show Filter	Clear Filter

Name ▾	Class	Family	Serial Number	Contact
ANV07	Server	Hardware.Server	111W23SSA	Ehrlich, Oliver
ANV38	Server	Hardware.Server	123AA89B	Ehrlich, Oliver
ANV39	Server	Hardware.Server	123AA234	Ehrlich, Oliver

Figure 8.2 Servers in Anvil Data Center

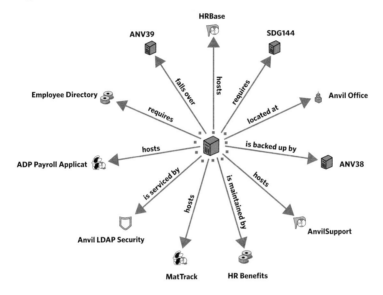

Figure 8.3 Visualization of Server ANV07

This is easily seen in Figure 8.2 and 8.3. These are screen shots from a CMDB application. Figure 8.2 is a listing of servers found in a very small data center. Figure 8.3 is a visualization of one of those servers. The list displays what you would see if you physically examined the data center. The visualization reveals the unseen relationships of just one of those servers.

The visualization tells us that shutting down one of the three servers at the vacant data center would cause four applications to fail. This is only the first level of dependencies. If we were to look at the secondary or tertiary dependencies, we might see more widespread effects. It is not surprising that even in organizations where changes are carefully controlled; changes are still at the root of most system failures. No wonder the first diagnostic question at the Service Desk is usually 'what changed?'

IT Initiatives are seldom as simple as moving a few servers, but agility and flexibility often determine their success. Providing IT services to a new facility requires careful planning. A flexible IT environment will easily expand to meet the need; a rigid environment will struggle. Agility and flexibility are a direct result of planning, and of understanding the IT environment. These efforts all require more than a superficial look at the IT environment. Where should the failover site for the web server farm be located? Does existing equipment have the capacity to support the new facility? Plans cannot be made without a set of blueprints for the infrastructure. A superficial or ad hoc view made up for the specific occasion, is not considered adequate planning.

It is necessary to review how some of the process tracks in the Service Support Subway uses (figure 8.4) the CMDB. Several tracks cross the Plan Junction since they require planning. Release Management, Change Management, and Configuration Management all use the CMDB as the center of the planning activities. Because the CMDB is designed to be the shared center, it is key to the smooth transfer of activities. For example, because both Change Management and Release Management are concerned with controlled changes and releases to the environment, both processes have inputs and outputs to the CMDB. A group of CIs that may be authorized for a change affect Release Management, which is responsible for the orderly deployment of those approved changes into production.

Without a CMDB, the two practices are forced to communicate via error-prone synchronization of their respective systems.

Do

A plan should relay what you want to do, but knowing what to do is useless if you don't actually do anything. The next stage in the journey is to execute your constructed plan. The CMDB plays a big role in this execution phase. In the planning stage, the CMDB may be used to project forward into the future; to show the planners how to construct their systems to meet future goals or to demonstrate what those systems would look like after they are deployed. During execution of that plan, a CMDB could reveal what the system is actually doing as the plan unrolls; keeping it on track to achieve the intended goals.

In IT, executing a plan is much more than plugging in a few cables, throwing some switches on and booting a few servers. Those activities may be enough to jumpstart a service, but they will seldom keep the service available for very long. A service requires support. ITIL describes best practices for support services. These practices make extensive use of a CMDB. In fact, Service Support is one of the basic reasons for establishing a CMDB.

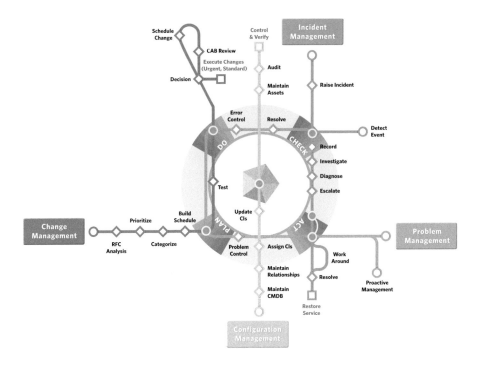

Figure 8.4 Service Support Subway

The main goal of Service Level Management is to keep the infrastructure functioning at a level of quality that meets the terms established in SLAs. Many enterprises have explicit SLAs, but even when there is no explicit SLA, user expectation forms an implicit SLA that must be met. Broadly, SLAs take two forms: IT SLAs that concentrate on specific IT metrics such as server uptime, and Business SLAs that focus more on availability and performance of business services. Typically, meeting business SLAs is dependent on meeting underlying IT SLAs.

A Service Desk exists to facilitate direction of resources to keep business services up and running, and to facilitate the resolution of those business service failures. The business user expects the services to be available and perform according to agreed service levels. An optimized Service Desk minimizes risk and maximizes return by assuring business SLAs with minimal resources. In order to meet this goal, the Service Desk has to make two important decisions. First, the Service Desk analyst must understand the impact of the incident on critical business services. After the impact is determined, a priority must be assigned for resolution of the incident. Assigning the correct impact to the incident minimizes the risk of ignoring incidents that affect critical business services. Assigning the proper priority to the incident ensures that enough resources are engaged to meet

SLAs, but also ensures that an excessive level of resource is not applied for resolution, which would divert resources from more business critical incidents that may be occurring.

After these decisions are made, the effort to restore a service to its agreed service level begins. The effort to restore a business service can take several directions. The incident may be transferred to an SME for resolution. A work-around may be instituted. The incident may be resolved directly by opening a change order to replace or upgrade a failing component. As part of the process of restoring service, the incident may be designated to be a problem that requires in-depth study to implement a long term solution.

When determining incident impact and priority, CMDB relationships and dependencies are used to identify the business services affected by a failing component. Technicians must understand that physical devices are only the means by which IT services are delivered and they should never confuse restoring a device with restoring the IT services upon which the business depends.

Leveraging the knowledge contained within a CMDB is a tremendous improvement over the ways of the past. In the past, incident priority was largely determined by the severity of the fault. For example, physical damage to a large data server may have been treated as a severe event because it affected an expensive asset and a large amount of data. However, the severity of the damage to the server is secondary. The real issue is around the SLA of the business services that are affected by the physical damage. These business service SLAs measure the business impact of the damage. An interruption to a 24/7 service at 2:00am may have an impact on business services; however severe physical damage at 2:00am may have less of an impact on the business than a minor power glitch causing a 10:00am interruption to a 9:00am-5;00pm service. Using the level of business impact to determine the priority of incidents optimizes the delivery of IT services that are critical to the business. Without the relationships and CI information housed within the CMDB, it is difficult for the Service Desk to prioritize incidents based on physical severity and business impact.

The CMDB is instrumental while traveling on the Incident Management track, when steps are taken to restore an interrupted service. Sometimes, when the cause of the incident is known, the response is straightforward, like replacing a drive (with an approved change request) and restoring a backup; but at other times, diagnosing and restoring an incident is more difficult.

Incidents often appear as an interruption or degradation in a service without a clear cause or a known resolution. When a business service is in trouble, and a CMDB is present, CMDB relationships and dependencies can trace the service interruption to the underlying physical devices and sub-services or processes that may have caused the service interruption. From there, the analyst or SME can identify a repair action or other response, to resolve the situation.

Business Continuity and incident impact are directly related. A major challenge in maintaining business continuity is determining what parts of the infrastructure must be protected, and to what degree. If we go back to the example in figures 8.2 and 8.3, moving the servers without examining the dependencies would result in the failure of four critical applications. If an incident occurred - for example, a hard disk crash on server ANV07 - proper evaluation of the impact of ANV07 would show those affected applications and take their SLAs into account. However, if we step back a moment, the CMDB not only displays this relationship, but it also shows that leaving ANV07 and its applications in a vulnerable position risks business continuity. ITSCM helps to ensure that an appropriate response can be provided, such as a redundant failover mechanism, or some other means of assuring IT service continuity.

The restoration of a business service frequently requires a change to the infrastructure. The change may be as simple as replacing a single failing component such as a defective network interface card, or it could entail a larger effort such as upgrading a LAN, setting up and configuring a firewall, or purchasing and installing new devices. ITIL suggests that these efforts are accompanied by an authorized Change Request.

When a change is authorized, the CMDB drives critical interaction between Change, Release and Configuration Management (figure 8.4). In ITIL, the CMDB serves as a proxy for the real infrastructure. Changes to a real CI or relationship are expected to occur in the proxy CMDB and the real infrastructure simultaneously, or even in the CMDB first. An example is a technician installing an additional gigabyte of RAM to a server. The installation would require an authorized change order and the change would have to be reflected in the CMDB.

The marriage between the real infrastructure and the CMDB proxy is often automated with discovery tools. Discovery tools can be based on several different technologies, each with their own advantages. By combining different technologies, the work required for identification of anomalies and maintenance of the CMDB can be reduced substantially whilst raising the level of accuracy of the data.

When the CMDB and the real infrastructure do not match, ITIL best practices advocate recording an incident, even though the real system may have been improved by the unofficial change. Although this may seem counter-intuitive, requiring an incident assures the alignment of the CMDB to the real infrastructure. The resolution of an incident might be to accept the unauthorized change to realign the CMDB accurately. Supporting a known system is easier than supporting a system that has to be examined each time a business service is degraded in order to determine what the interruption might be.

ITIL assumes that the CMDB represents the infrastructure in a known working state. When there is a discrepancy between the contents of the CMDB and the real environment, the viability of the infrastructure is unknown. The infrastructure may be working well, but the only way to be sure is to restore it to the known working state as described in the CMDB.

Comparing the failing system to the known working system described in the CMDB is a rapid route to business service restoration and is frequently cited as justifying the effort in setting up and maintaining a CMDB.

Check
The Check phase of the Deming Cycle (sometimes called the study phase) also makes use of the CMDB. At this point in the cycle, an initiative has been in motion long enough to evaluate successes and failures and identify improvements to the service. This is the feedback stage.

When the results of a change are studied, whether it is a complex change like launching a new accounting system or a standard change like replacing a cooling fan, the study usually begins with a 'before and after' look at the situation. A CMDB provides the before and after view of the IT environment. This is similar to comparing the real infrastructure to the CMDB. The before and after views can take two forms: a pair of snapshots or an incremental record. Snapshots capture the state of the system at two instances in time. The incremental view records each step in moving back from the end point to the starting point. Both approaches are useful: snapshots are broad; steps are detailed.

With an understanding of the changes to the system, the checking phase can look in detail at what the modified system does well and what not so well, as controlled by Configuration Management (figure 8.4). Consider the simple cooling fan replacement. The CMDB tells you that the fan was replaced. If a Service Desk is federated with the CMDB, the record of incidents on the piece of equipment (represented as CI in the CMDB) that was repaired will reveal the mean time between failure (MTBF) and the mean time to repair (MTR) for the device. A device monitor that is federated with the CMDB will yield similar information. One hopes that all metrics will have improved, but the knowledge that metrics have not improved can be as valuable as confirmation that the plan was beneficial.

Problem Management cannot perform a thorough root cause analysis of an incident without the visibility provided by the CMDB (figure 8.4). For example, MTBF and MTR are interesting, but we can go further. The

MTBF and MTR of a CI can be measured, but the metrics have business impact only when they affect business services. The easiest way to trace the business impact of a metric on a CI is to consult the CMDB. The CMDB can be used to evaluate the impact; that is, which business services have improved or degraded as a result of this change, similar to evaluating the impact of support services at the Service Desk. If important business services have improved, the replacement was probably a good use of resources. On the other hand, if the replacement caused no improvement, or even degraded services, the change process could be problematic and this impact information may be used to guide an overhaul of the Change Management process.

The CMDB will provide similar guidance in larger projects. On a larger scale, guidance from the CMDB can have more significance than changes on a small scale, but the same principles apply.

Act
The Act phase of the Deming Cycle uses the facts gathered from the checking phase. This use can take several different directions. If the study reveals that the original plan was ideal, IT may decide to standardize on the plan and implement it on a wider scale in the enterprise. If the plan was good, but could have been better, an improved plan could be implemented as a result. If the plan was harmful, then it can be scrapped or overhauled.

The action phase completes the Deming Cycle, and the cycle begins again. The continuous cycle addresses new challenges as they arrive and improves responses to existing challenges. IT professionals are often tempted to apply continuous improvement disciplines like the Deming Cycle to their IT environment without regard to business services. There are many tools and disciplines that help enterprises to improve the quality of services, but there are few that are as useful as a CMDB for applying technical improvement to business services. At every phase of the cycle, a CMDB provides the foundation of business service facts for continuous improvement.

The objective of the Release Management process is to oversee the controlled distribution of software and hardware components into the live environment. The Release Management process provides a structured approach to the management of releases into the IT infrastructure, from initial policy and release planning, through design, building and release configuration, to testing, release distribution and installation. The main components controlled by Release Management include in-house developed or packaged software applications, software provided by suppliers (such as software patches and operating system versions), hardware and user manuals, and documentation.

Sound Release Management activities increase the quality of a production environment, by ensuring formal procedures when implementing new versions. Release Management works closely with Change Management to build and implement changes from authorized RFCs. Unlike Change Management, which focuses on change verification and control, Release Management is concerned with the actual implementation of changes. Since a release is a set of new or changed CIs, the process is also closely aligned with Configuration Management to update configuration details about hardware and software components and their relationships. This information is maintained within the CMDB.

Release Management is responsible for legal and contractual obligations related to the hardware and software used by the organization. To meet these obligations and protect IT assets, Release Management works to establish definitive, secure and auditable environments for hardware (in what is known as a Definitive Hardware Store, or DHS) and software (in what is known as the Definitive Software Library, or DSL).

Before reviewing the Release Management process (figure 9.1), it is necessary to consider important relationships with other ITIL processes. To be effective, Release Management should always work closely and integrate with Configuration Management and Change Management, while leveraging Problem Management and the Service Desk function.

- **Change Management.** Change Management provides information and recommendations to Release Management on the content and scheduling of releases. Release Management is then responsible for implementing the agreed releases. Because of this close association, a Release Manager is often a member of the CAB which is involved in establishing the organization's release policy. Although Release Management oversees the details of the rollout of a change, Change Management is ultimately responsible for it.

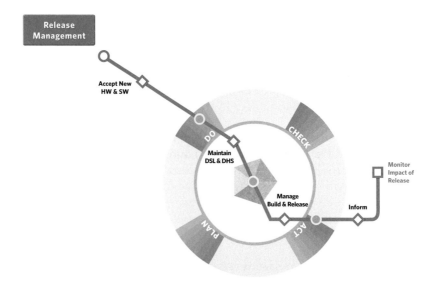

Figure 9.1 Release Management Process Line

- **Configuration Management.** When new versions of software are released and added to the DSL, process integration must ensure that details are also added to the CMDB, of which the DSL is a Configuration Item. Similarly, when new or changed hardware is rolled out, the CMDB should be updated. The CMDB should always contain the current status information on all authorized software and hardware, and it is used to ensure that only the correct components are included in a release. Release Management may use various services of Configuration Management during the implementation of a Release (eg a configuration audit to ensure that the target environment is as expected for the release).

- **Problem Management and the Service Desk.** At the end of the successful distribution and installation of a new release, Release Management provides Problem Management with vital information. For example:
  - Any known errors or problems introduced by the new release should be documented so that Service Desk staff can better support it.
  - Problem Management and Service Desk staff should be informed of the new release - and be trained in new or revised support procedures - so that they can support its use in the live environment.

Problem Management teams are also often involved in identifying known errors that will lead to RFCs and eventually to new releases.

- **IT Continuity Management**. During the Release Management process, release teams not only assess the risk of the rollout (ie the operational impacts), but they must also examine the effects of a possible future disaster. When a new release is rolled out, the continuity plans should be reviewed, updated as necessary, and tested to ensure optimal business support.

The major activities within Release Management include: Release Policy and Planning, Design, Build and Configure, Testing and Release Acceptance, Rollout Planning, Communication and Training, and Installation.

HARDWARE & SOFTWARE

Release Management must be engaged early in the development lifecycle, before new hardware and software components can be accepted into the live environment. Ideally, any development that results in changes to the production environment should be controlled by Change Management, with all RFCs reviewed and approved by both development and operations and managed through a single change process. This approach improves communication and increases the number of successful releases.

To optimize the effectiveness of the process, it is also important to build policies defining how and when releases are configured, and to make recommendations addressing any concerns and issues, such as the level of IT infrastructure controlled by Release Management, release blackout periods, back-out plans and testing, naming conventions and documentation.

Since Release Management affects every process area in a live environment, preparation and planning requires a structured project management approach. Every release is a project with a lifecycle that starts with an RFC and ends with a post implementation review. And since the process manages many releases simultaneously, ITIL recommends the use of a formal project management methodology (such as PRINCE2) to increase the chance of success for every release, and for Release Management as a whole. Since many development groups adopt project management disciplines, the Release Management process should adopt similar principles to improve the co-ordination of activities between operations and software development.

MAINTAIN DSL & DHS

MANAGE BUILD & RELEASE

The next stage of the Release Management process involves the design, construction and configuration of a potential release using standard procedures in a controlled or reproducible manner. The output of this activity should be a release, complete with installation instructions, a test plan and a blackout plan stored in the DSL and DHS. A release may be based on components developed in-house, or purchased and configured. Installation and configuration instructions should always form part of the release, and should be treated as CIs under the control of Change Management and Configuration Management. From a software perspective, this process activity is often called 'build' management, which can be extremely time-consuming and error-prone if performed manually. Fortunately, technology is available to automate procedures and ensure that software executables are created in the same way every time. During this stage, hardware components may need to be assembled, and similar procedures need to be applied to ensure reproducible configurations. Here again, technology can be used to automate the installation of operating system and application software.

A back-out plan should be produced toward the end of this stage to define the activities that need to be performed if something goes wrong with the release. While Change Management may have responsibility for drawing up back-out plans for each change, Release Management must ensure that all back-outs can be practically applied. There are two common approaches to back-outs, and a combination of both may be used:

- First, a failed release is reversed. This step is critical for a full release, and preferable for a partial or delta release.
- Secondly, if a release cannot be rolled back, disaster recovery plans are initiated to recover service.

The next Release Management activity involves acceptance testing in a controlled test environment. Lack of adequate testing is the most common cause of failure of all releases. To avoid this situation before implementation, any release should undergo both functional user testing and operational testing by IT staff. Once development testing is completed, the release is logged in the DSL, and the development team should update the known-error database to reflect any errors identified during development testing. The release is then checked out of the DSL for testing in the controlled environment by the operations team. Operational testing is an area that is often neglected, and the IT organization needs to ensure rigorous testing of technical operations, performance within the IT infrastructure and other operational aspects. These tests should also include tests on installation procedures and back-out plans. A formal list of acceptance of each step is submitted to Change Management for authorization, with the final stage being authorization of the release for implementation.

At this point, Release Management works closely with Change Management to determine a schedule for the implementation and post implementation review, and publishes to the Change Management FSC. When final authorization is provided, Release Management will then implement the change into the live production environment on the date and time specified.

If a release is rejected, it should be rescheduled through Change Management. Rejected releases should be tracked and reported through Change Management as failed changes. Failed releases and their impact on operations and support staff resources should also be monitored. The outputs of the release testing and acceptance stage include:

- tested installation procedures
- tested release components
- tested back-out procedures
- known defects to be carried forward into the live environment
- test results
- support documentation, including the system overview
- updated support procedures
- diagnostic aids
- operating and administration instructions
- contingency and back-out plans
- a training schedule for Service Management, support staff and customers
- acceptance test documentation signed by all relevant parties
- and authorization to implement the release (conducted through Change Management as discussed above)

Following the testing stage, rollout planning should be performed to add details of the exact installation process developed and the agreed implementation plan. Rollout planning involves:

- producing an exact, detailed timetable of events, as well as who will do what (ie a resource plan)
- listing the CIs to install and decommission, with details on the method of disposal for any redundant equipment and software
- documenting an action plan by site, citing the business objectives that the release is addressing and noting any time zone implications on the overall plans (eg an international organization may well not have a

single common release window when none of its systems are being used throughout the world)
- producing release notes and communications to end users
- planning communication
- developing purchasing plans
- acquiring hardware and software; since this step often involves the acquisition and deployment of numerous high-value assets, the rollout plan should include the procedures to be followed prior to rollout and the mechanisms to trace their deployment during the implementation (which could involve the use of asset tags or other electronically readable labels)
- scheduling meetings for managing staff and groups involved in the release

Before releases can be distributed and installed, customers and appropriate support staff should be advised on the release details and how this affects them. This is normally accomplished through a series of joint training sessions and release acceptance activities. Any changes that need to be made during distribution and installation should be communicated to all parties to set their expectations. This activity normally includes running a series of rollout planning meetings with all of the stakeholders to ensure that the plans are properly reviewed, with responsibilities agreed upon and understood.

Changes to hardware or software support contracts may also need to be communicated to the relevant staff. This is the responsibility of the Service Desk, but Release Management may be better positioned to undertake the detailed communication.

Release distribution and installation manages the purchase, storage, transport, delivery and handover of software and hardware. The processes for procurement, storage, dispatch, receipt and disposal of goods should ensure that equipment is delivered safely to its destination in its expected state. Checks on the receipt of goods against supporting delivery documentation are required for Configuration Management.

Wherever possible, automated tools for software distribution should be used to expedite the installation, increase quality and free up resources. These tools also will facilitate verification of successful releases and provide automated mechanisms to back-out failed or partially completed releases.

Installing the software releases is the final step in the process. Here, it is common to distribute a new version of a software application to a target installation so that it remains dormant until activated. This should be accomplished by following the tested installation procedures, and may involve running automated installation routines or other one-offs. To ensure a smooth rollout, an automated check of the target platform is required so as to ensure that it meets hardware and software prerequisites. Here again, automated technologies can assist with the process.

The CMDB should be updated following installation or disposal of hardware or software, to ensure that it reflects the final position after a release. It may also be necessary to retrieve old versions of software that have been superseded, to prevent software license rules from being violated.

After a successful installation, the Configuration Management records should be updated with the location and the owner of the hardware and software. This will assist support staff to locate equipment and resolve any subsequent incidents and problems. Finally, Change Management is notified and takes responsibility for conducting Post Implementation Reviews and closing the associated RFC.

9.1 Optimizing Release Management

Release Management involves implementing approved changes into the live or production environment with minimal negative impact on the business. Release Management works best when integrated with Change Management and Configuration Management to drive continuous improvement and the quality of IT services. Release Management works with Change Management to ensure that only approved changes are implemented, and with Configuration Management to ensure that records are updated and accurate.

9.2 Leveraging Technology for Process Automation

Many technological solutions can automate Release Management process activities and integrate the closely related processes of Change Management and Configuration Management. Examples include:

- **Operational Change and Configuration Management Tools.** Release Management should make use of Change Management tools that can record information about planned and scheduled changes. Change Management tools hold information about the releases, with links to the changes that they implement and links to the Configuration items that are affected by the releases. A good change management solution will allow tracking and auditing of changes and the releases that implement them, together with facilities to authorize various phases electronically during the release lifecycle. Solutions in this category also allow hardware and software CIs to be recorded in the CMDB with status updates as the release progresses.

- **Software Change and Configuration Management (SCCM).** These tools manage different versions of software source code during its development. Of particular importance is the ability of these tools to determine the impact of changes on other parts of the system. Ideally, SCCM tools should include build management capability, whereby program compilations and links are performed in the correct sequence.
- **Software Distribution.** Enterprise-capable software distribution tools are helpful, featuring assured delivery, integrity checking, back-out and restart capabilities, and a variety of distribution methods designed to make the best use of network designs and available bandwidth.
- **IT Asset Management.** These solutions can perform hardware and software audits and ensure that target release platforms are capable of supporting release rollouts.
- **Reporting.** Mechanisms to report KPIs on the Release Management process are important. At a minimum, reports and service dashboards should be capable of proving the following:
  - releases built and implemented on schedule
  - accurate distribution of releases to all remote sites
  - the number of major and minor releases per reporting period
  - the number of problems in the live environment that can be attributed to new releases, which need only be measured during the first few months of a new release's life, classified by root cause, (eg 'wrong version of file' or 'missing files')
  - the number of new, changed and deleted objects introduced by the new release
  - known Error effectiveness (number of Incidents tied to Known Errors)
  - the number of releases completed in the agreed timescales, which requires the central Release Management function to publish predefined targets (service levels agreements) for software distributions and other common tasks

9.3 Benefits of Release Management

- improved quality of services due to better integration of hardware, software and documentation which are part of a provides services
- better overview of dependencies between services and within services
- fewer calls to the Service Desk
- increase in the amount of first-contact fixes, due to an up-to-date CMDB and embedded Change Management supporting Release Management
- increased control on over and under licensing, ultimately resulting in major cost savings
- better planning of releases which leads to less disturbance among the business users for new release rollouts
- improved quality and professionalism at the Service Desk
- facilitates optimal business support environments

9.4 Avoiding Problems

- Any activity (Design, Building, Testing, Training and Communication, Implementation) must ensure that all release criteria have been met and are in line with the business objectives and service agreements. Sign-off should take place at the end of each phase. Random audits may be necessary to ensure that the release criteria sign-offs are being met rigorously. Requirements of the Service Desk should not be taken lightly. The Service desk must be involved in the sign-off process.
- The supporting deliverables of the release that directly affect the Service Desk must be complete. This includes thorough documentation and complete and accurate escalation lists.
- The Service Desk should receive formal training on any new release or major upgrade. This training may be developed in-house or provided by a third party in advance of the release.
- Compliance with security policies is an important consideration. The release process must ensure that established security policies are incorporated in all phases of the release. This will minimize any adverse security issues. In some organizations, an IT Security representative is assigned to a release project to ensure compliance with security policy.

Service Delivery

CHAPTER 10 Availability Management

The objective of Availability Management is to provide a cost-effective and defined level of service availability that enables the business to reach its objectives. Availability Management can be met through process, technology and people, resource planning and implementation. In general, Availability Management is the process of ensuring IT Services are available when required, have the capacity to recover quickly and are not liable to malfunction.

Availability Management is about understanding and meeting the needs of the business. Meeting these needs is accomplished by managing the availability, serviceability, maintainability and reliability of IT services.

- **Availability** - services provided according to agreed service times with the customer, response times, etc.
- **Serviceability** - the expected availability of a component where a service is provided by a third party supplier
- **Maintainability** - the ease with which an IT component can be maintained (which can be both remedial and preventative)
- **Reliability** - the time for which an IT component can be expected to perform under specific conditions without failure

Good Availability Management is also about proactively designing for the availability of the IT infrastructure, as documented in SLAs, rather than reactively trying to make services available. Availability Management also serves to make services available at optimum costs in order to support the business objectives.

This business and IT alignment creates the environment needed to maximize the availability of IT related components, thereby increasing customer satisfaction, and empowering the business to design for availability rather than fire fight to make services available, reactively. Availability management is also the cornerstone of Information Security in ITIL, being one of the three major building blocks (confidentiality, integrity, availability) of any security strategy.

The benefits of Availability Management include:

- reduced cost of downtime
- systems are managed according to business availability targets
- there is a greater level of control over IT systems
- new systems are produced according to the availability requirements rather than designing availability around

- an increased level of support for the core business operations
- a reduction in the level of reactive support for IT systems

There are a number of critical activities of Availability Management that this chapter focuses on. These activities include planning for IT/Business Plans, new services, design and recovery requirements; measuring availability, reliability and maintainability metrics; and automated monitoring and improving IT services against measurements.

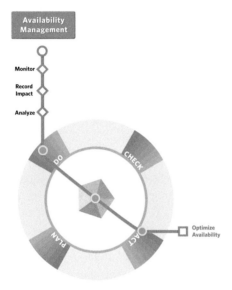

Figure 10.1 Availability Management Process Line

The key activities of Availability Management are represented in figure 10.1, and include:

- Monitor
- Record an Impact
- Analyze
- Maintain Resilience and security

The Availability Management subway line crosses all of the major Service Delivery lines because of its focus on proper design, implementation, measurement and management of the IT Infrastructure availability to ensure that the stated business requirements for availability are consistently met.

Availability Management should create and maintain a proactive availability plan aimed at improving the overall availability of IT services and infrastructure components, and ensuring that any capability gaps are quickly identified and rectified. By traveling along this line, and by continuously optimizing activities, IT organizations can reduce the frequency and duration of incidents that impact IT Availability, and thereby help to achieve the process objective of ensuring IT services are available when required.

The journey of Availability Management begins with monitoring the current state of IT service availability. This stage involves determining what infrastructure components should be monitored, setting up a monitoring plan and identifying appropriate monitoring tools. Key tasks at this stage include collecting and monitoring key metrics of infrastructure availability, including:

- **Availability** - accumulated downtime over given periods of time
- **Reliability** - the frequency of downtime
- **Maintainability** - how well the organization maintains IT services in an operational state
- **Serviceability** - identical to maintainability, but involves monitoring external service providers

During the monitoring stage of Availability Management it is critical to measure as much information as possible, so as to be able to verify SLAs, identify problem areas, and present proposals for availability improvements. All good IT Service Management requires ongoing monitoring and reporting on the process environment, and the Availability Management journey is no different.

Appropriate monitoring will help identify incidents and provide the information to anticipate, or predict IT failures, thereby empowering IT staff to act in a preventative rather than a reactive manner. Automation of monitoring activities will improve the IT organizations ability to control the environment by providing accurate and detailed reports. The organizational benefits include minimizing the impact on perceived quality, improved user satisfaction and enhanced business reputation.

In order to support the monitoring of service availability, monitoring applications can collect the data and automatically correlate that data against pre defined thresholds that reflect the true business, user and IT perspectives. This data can then be used in trend analysis, helping to identify unacceptable levels of services and promoting a dialog to correct them rapidly.

Even with the best hardware, systems and software failures will occur within the operational infrastructure, resulting in deviations from normal service. Once we understand and can measure availability from our monitoring activities, the next objective is to align any outage to an IT service and document the impact of the outage. The outage, or unavailability impact, will allow us to identify the infrastructure components causing availability problems and help us to understand where we may be incurring excessive costs, unplanned expenditure and additional costs charged by suppliers. It is important to note that sometimes an overlooked area of Availability Management is the management of suppliers, since few organizations manage and maintain their entire infrastructure. For example, a call centre or Service Desk is often externally managed. These supplier relationships should include associated SLAs because these are vital to managing the availability of the complete service and understanding the impact of unavailability.

The IT organization traditionally has extensive usage and availability information, although often not organized in a format that can be utilized for good availability analysis. At this stage on the Availability Management line, it is important to identify, analyze and manage the current data to assess and identify areas of improvement. In performing a structured analysis, the objective is to create an availability matrix with the relevant information about provided services and components.

To accomplish this task a broad spectrum of methods and techniques are available:

- **Component Failure Impact Analysis (CFIA)** can assist identification of key components and their roles in each service.
- **Fault Tree Analysis (FTA)** can be used to identify the chain of events leading to failure.
- **CCTA Risk Analysis and Management Method (CRAMM)** provides the means to identify justifiable countermeasures to protect IT services against performance and security breaches.

- **Service Outage Analysis (SOA)** is a technique used to identify the causes of faults, investigate the IT organizations effectiveness, and provide recommendations for improvement.
- **The Technical Observation Post (TOP)** method is based on a dedicated team of IT specialists who will investigate a single aspect of availability when routine applications provide insufficient information.

These methods can provide inputs to availability calculations, based on pre-defined metrics, which can be used as input to the service availability agreements that will be included in an SLA for a related IT service agreed with its customers.

Tools and best practices exist today that rapidly detect service degradation and ensure systems resilience before users are impacted by IT service outages. The mission of Availability Management is to leverage the information from monitoring and analysis in order to establish a secure environment to support sustainable services. It is important to realize that security and reliability are closely linked. For example, insufficient security planning and design can affect the availability of the service. During the service availability planning stage and development of availability plan, security issues must be considered. The impact on the service provisioning, such as authorized access to secure areas and critical authorizations, should be addressed.

10.1 Optimizing the Availability Management Journey

Successful Availability Management depends on the business clearly defining their availability objectives and service requirements. Optimization of the Availability Management process is possible with the integration of SLM. Optimizing the Availability Management journey should include defining SLAs with availability components, since SLM will serve to formalize the relationship between IT and customers of IT, thereby demonstrating the benefits of IT services availability. An example quality metric based on the core objective of Availability Management is to measure the % of service availability to ensure that it is within an SLA negotiated requirement.

When implemented with relevant and meaningful metrics, Availability Management can influence the way in which IT services are designed, implemented and managed. By understanding the business processes and how IT supports those processes you are able to increase customer satisfaction by eliminating constraints that can affect service performance which will, in turn, make a positive impact on the culture of your organization.

10.2 Avoiding Availability Management Issues and Problems

Availability Management often suffers from misunderstandings that may inhibit its establishment and deployment in an organization. The most common barriers include:

- Perception. There is a difference in the level of availability of 'systems' and the availability of 'services' that is often misunderstood; for example, IT may report to the business that the percentage availability of the Lotus Notes system is 97.5% and the availability of NT Servers is 99%, and think that they are doing a great job. However, if the availability of the 'Printing Service' is at 65%, then the perception by the business would be that IT is not providing the required level of availability and perhaps outsourcing is an option.
- Relevant Availability metrics should be presented to the business and not simply raw IT availability data.
- Lack of understanding of how Availability Management will make a significant improvement is significant, especially when disciplines such as Incident Management, Problem Management and Change Management are being implemented, without looking at the bigger picture.
- If current levels of Availability are considered 'acceptable' managers may see little value of embarking on the Availability Management journey.
- IT staff may see IT availability as the responsibility of all senior managers and offer resistance over who will be empowered and soon responsible for managing IT service availability; it is therefore important to communicate the value of appointing an overall accountable role.

11 Capacity Management

The objective of Capacity Management is to ensure that the current state of an IT infrastructure functions to meet the current and future business demands, and also to ensure that capacity of IT services is utilized in a cost effective manner.

Capacity Management has a number of activities into which the other ITIL processes provide inputs. For example, the Incident Management process will inform Capacity Management about incidents due to capacity problems. The outputs of Capacity Management also support many other processes. For example, Capacity Management can inform Change Management about the need for additional capacity, and the potential impact of a service on current capacity levels. These integration points are visually represented in the Capacity Management process line (figure 11.1). According to ITIL, the key activities for Capacity Management are:

- **Performance monitoring**; performance metrics, thresholds, throughput
- **Tuning**: optimizing existing resources
- **Planning**: establishing capacity plans to define infrastructure requirements in line with business operations
- **Defining policies**: recognizing and establishing constraints around system operations
- **Demand Management**: understanding current and future resource demands

This chapter focuses on these activities, locally grouped as stations en route to the process objective, which in this case, is ensuring that IT operations (the current Service Delivery) and IT Infrastructure (the means of delivering service) support the future capacity of IT services that are required by the business (the required Service Delivery) in the most cost effective manner. It is important to keep in mind, however, that Capacity Management is also about understanding the potential for Service Delivery, so new technology should be leveraged and, if appropriate, used to deliver the services required by the business, cost effectively.

There are a number of stops on the Capacity Management process line:

- **Demand Management:** responsible for ensuring that the capacity of the IT infrastructure matches the evolving demands of the business in the most cost-effective and timely manner. Capacity Management influences the demand for resources, perhaps in conjunction with Financial Management. Capacity Management is always performing a balancing act such as cost against capacity, for example:

- the need to ensure that processing capacity that is purchased is not only cost justifiable in terms of business need, but also the need to make the most efficient use of those resources, and supply against demand
- making sure that the available supply of processing power matches the demands made on it by the business, both now and in the future. It may also be necessary to manage or influence the demand for a particular resource.

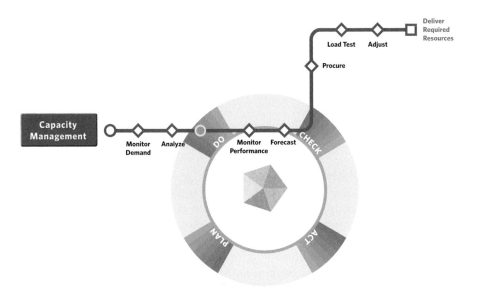

Figure 11.1 Capacity Management Process Line

- **Monitor demand:** monitoring and reporting of capacity performance and throughput of IT services and the supporting infrastructure components on a consistent and ongoing basis
- **Tuning:** undertaking required tuning activities to make the most efficient use of existing resources
- **Analyze**: taking input from performance management, resource management, workload management, demand management, and application sizing, in order to understand the demands currently being made for IT resources and producing forecasts for future requirements
- **New services:** production of a Capacity Plan on an annual basis that will enable the IT service provider to provide services of the quality defined in SLAs.

Before we move on to the detailed descriptions of each of the process activities, it is useful to review how Capacity Management consists of a number of sub-processes, within which there are various activities. The sub-processes of Capacity Management are:

11.1 Business Capacity Management:

- This sub-process is responsible for ensuring that the future business requirements for IT services are considered, planned and implemented in a timely fashion. This timeliness can be achieved by analyzing data on current resource utilization, to forecast and model future requirements. Future requirements come from business plans that indicate the need for new services and needed improvements or growth in existing systems. As with many ITIL activities, successful Business Capacity Management involves close collaboration between IT and the business.

11.2 Service Capacity Management:

- The focus of this sub-process is the management of the performance of the live, operational IT services that end-users utilize to perform daily functions. This sub-process is focused on end-to-end services rather than individual infrastructure components. Here, IT must first look at the overall service in order to determine the business needs before examining individual infrastructure components. If analysis is performed on each IT component first, then the organization runs the risk of investing resources where they are impacting the overall provision of service. Service Capacity Management is essential, since it enables IT to develop close links with the business once again.

11.3 Resource Capacity Management:

- The focus in this sub-process is the management of the individual components of the IT infrastructure. This is the traditional IT view, and is responsible for ensuring that all IT components that support a particular IT service are closely monitored and measured, and that exercises are constantly performed to improve service capacity requirements. Again, a structured and top-down approach to Capacity Management ensures closer business alignment, and enables the prioritization of capacity investments to be based on business needs.

The Capacity Management journey (like many of the other journeys) begins with monitoring your current state; in this case, your current service capacity state.

MONITOR DEMAND

Monitoring demand is about understanding where you are now with your current capabilities in supporting your users demand for capacity. Monitoring of capacity demand levels can tell you how many users are impacting your resources and in what ways. It also provides valuable information on the current capacity levels of resources, so that IT will know how to support new services that will be introduced into the environment, and how SLAs are going to be affected. Demand monitoring activities are important because they allow you to collect relevant data for specific components of services that you can present to the business to help them to make smart and effective decisions. It is usually a good idea to make decisions based on what you know to be true.

Utilization of each resource and service is monitored on an on-going basis to ensure the optimum use of the hardware and software resources, that all agreed service levels can be achieved, and that business volumes are as expected. The monitoring activity of Capacity Management includes:

- CPU & memory Utilization
- I/O rates
- device utilization
- due length
- storage utilization
- transaction rate
- packet loss
- response time
- burst rate
- bandwidth utilization

And can trigger typical capacity initiatives such as:

- archiving
- work load balancing
- upgrade projections
- tolerance levels
- restrictions of usage
- data storage tuning

Monitored data can include CPU utilization or transaction response times, to name two, but the key thing to remember is that there is a difference between the information collected around managing capacity (throughput) and the data needed to monitor performance (response time). Business decisions are driven by an understanding of both. Technology can enhance monitoring of thresholds and normal service levels; for example, if thresholds are exceeded, automated alerts can notify the Service Desk that there is a deviation from the expected level of capacity, and the appropriate escalation procedure can be followed.

So regardless of whichever sub-process (Business, Service or Resource Capacity Management) is involved, monitoring of IT resources is a key activity of the Capacity Management process that should be performed in order to help achieve the goal that capacity meets the requirements of the business.

The data collected from the current demand monitoring should be analyzed to identify trends from which the normal utilization and service level, or baseline, can be established.
Some key metrics for Capacity Management include:

- processor usage by workload and application
- relative resource consumption
- min/max transactions per second
- online response times and trends
- utilization statistics
- business usage trends
- processor and I/O usage trends
- network usage trends
- workload trends and forecasts
- growth forecasts

Analyzing this data allows trends to appear; we know the importance of trends from the Problem Management journey. Trending allows for understanding what is considered 'normal' which serves as a benchmark to compare any deviation from 'normal'. Any deviation from expected utilization levels, thresholds or response times can be immediately detected and acted upon. The beauty of capacity monitoring and analysis is that the information collected can be used to predict future behaviors. And this is where technology can help, by predicting future resource usage, and monitoring actual business growth against predicted growth. With the information analyzed, decisions can be made to improve performance or make more efficient use of system resources. A way to improve these capabilities is by 'tuning' and is best supported by technology to perform such techniques, such as work load balancing.

Once monitoring and analyzing the data is underway, a way of storing the information is required. This storage requirement is where the Capacity Database (CDB) comes into focus. The Capacity Management process collects data from a variety of hardware platforms and software applications that may be widely distributed, so technology helps to organize that information and make it available in the CDB. Make sure that the maintenance of CDB data is controlled by the Change Management process, so that Changes are considered for their impact on the CDB.

MONITOR PERFORMANCE

At the initial Monitor stop where we first boarded the Capacity Line, we touched briefly on monitoring performance; specifically monitoring response times. A major intersection here is with Service Level Management, since SLAs usually make reference to expected response times; specifically user expected response times for service restoration, escalation and resolution. The monitoring of response times is a complex process, which is why technology can greatly support this activity. Supporting technology can include network monitoring systems, distributed agent monitoring systems or by incorporating specific code within client and server applications software that allows for real time monitoring of user performance.

FORECAST

Forecasting activities allow the business to predict future growth intelligently and plan accordingly for capacity. This can be done in a variety of ways depending on the technology. Armed with this forward thinking, the business can decide that it wants to double the amount of web based users of a service, for example, and will be able to know the direct costs associated with the new usage consumption rates based on current data and growth patterns. If the forecast on capacity identifies a requirement for increased resources, this then becomes an input to the IT budget cycle. Monitoring and analyzing of expected service levels will allow for forecast of future breaches of service targets if capacity is not planned for by understanding the current state. Some forecasting techniques include:

Tuning

The analysis of the monitored data may identify areas of the configuration that could be tuned to better utilize the system resource or improve the performance of the particular service.

Implementation

The objective of this activity is to introduce to the live operation service, any changes that have been identified by the monitoring, analysis and tuning activities.

Storage of Capacity Management Data

Data in the Capacity Management Database is stored and used by all the sub-processes of Capacity Management because it is a repository that holds a number of different data types, including business, service, technical, financial and utilization data.

Modeling

A prime objective of Capacity Management is to predict the behavior of IT Services under a given volume and variety of work. Modeling is an activity that can be used to beneficial effect in any of the sub-processes of Capacity Management.

Application Sizing

The primary objective of application sizing is to estimate the resource requirements to support a proposed application change or new application, to ensure that it meets its required service levels. To achieve this objective, application sizing has to be an integral part of the applications lifecycle.

11.4 Production of the Capacity Plan

The prime objective is to produce a plan that documents the current levels of resource utilization and service performance, and after consideration of the business strategy and plans, forecasts the future requirements for resources to support the IT Services that underpin the business activities.

The key takeaway: forecasting allows for 'what if' scenarios to be implemented without affecting the current state, but provides information to budget and plan for the future based on true data. Before leaving the Forecast station, it is important to give closer examination to the Capacity Plan. The Capacity Plan is a forward looking strategy based on forecasting, but also looks backwards at the data from monitoring and analysis to accurately predict growth and capacity requirements. This plan should align the current IT capacity to future workloads, performance and Service Level Requirements, and align to the goals of the business. The development of the capacity plan comes from data about the current environment including the results from load testing or the data collected from modeling tools. In a nutshell, the capacity plan includes management summaries around business, service and resource capacity information, cost information, and service target agreements; all of the information compiled through monitoring and analysis in order to forecast future business lines which will include new services.

PROCURE

Capacity Management can help with designing and procurement of new services, and crosses an intersection with Availability Management where, as future capacity requirements are defined, Availability Management works to ensure the proper design.

Demand Management

The prime objective of Demand Management is to influence the demand for computing resources and the use of those resources. In other words, the Demand Design and procurement of new services should be based on the requirements of the business and on an understanding of the capabilities to support those requirements. This is possible when there is an understanding of the current capacity. Capacity Management provides the business with the information they need in order to make financial decisions such as which components to upgrade and when to purchase new hardware to support future capacity requirements. Capacity Management should be involved in the design of new services and make recommendations for the procurement of hardware and software, where performance and/or Capacity are factors. In the interest of balancing cost and Capacity, the Capacity Management process obtains the costs of proposed solutions and the business decides 'to procure or not to procure' based on that information.

LOAD TEST

The next stop ensures that things do not 'break' when all applications are running concurrently and at the transaction level, identified as 'full load'. This information will provide an ability to support the business when they are forecasting and drafting their timelines for new application service offerings to support a business initiative such as a new web application for online banking, for example. This involves scenario testing and technology which can greatly assist the creation of 'what if' scenarios as in 'modeling' activities, which can in turn supply the data to support the best plan of action.

Following the Deming Cycle of continuous improvement model, at the Adjust station, adjustments are being made to systems to ensure that they are running optimally after the various load tests have been carried out. New services are procured and before those services are released (best practice Change and Release Management) into the environment activities such as load testing are conducted, and then systems are adjusted as data is received. This optimizes the ability of Capacity Management to meet its goal of cost effective supply of capacity to match the needs of the business – this is smart Capacity Management.

Management is all about manipulation. For example, you may want to manipulate usage because your current capacity levels are insufficient and this is your work-around. Or, you have decided to create a policy that manipulates usage because that meets the requirements of the business and there is no budget to increase capacity levels. Either way, it is an intelligent way to maintain services that are critical to the business and maximize the benefit of Capacity Management.

But smart Demand Management is about understanding the current state; which services are utilizing certain resources and at what level. Then decisions can be made as to whether it is even possible to manipulate the use of that resource. Manipulation or influence on the use of services can either be a physical restriction or a financial restriction. Physical restrictions can be supported by technology to limit the number of concurrent users of a resource. A financial restriction might be: increase the cost of one resource which will make utilization of another unrestricted resource, more attractive.

Again, the key to successful Demand Management is to understand the business requirements, the demands on IT Services, and communicate to your customers.

11.5 Optimizing the Capacity Management Journey

The primary role of the Capacity Management process is to ensure that sufficient IT Capacity exists at all times, to provide Customers with the agreed level of services. Technology exists to help enhance the Capacity Management process by automating the many activities that have already been discussed.
The benefits of Capacity Management include:

- spending money on the right things at the right time
- utilizing existing systems in a more effective way within budget
- proactively manage systems to reduce incidents and problems
- increased customer satisfaction
- the ability to anticipate

11.6 Avoiding Capacity Management Problems

- Informal or immature service management processes may exist that are key inputs to Capacity Management. For example, SLAs may exist that did not consider the input of Capacity Management, which therefore leads to under or over utilization of some of the capacity resources.
- An IT organization may view Capacity Management as a responsibility of all senior managers and therefore deny budget for a Capacity Manager role; so no one is accountable as a result.
- If there is a process owner appointment, it is important to ensure that they receive the appropriate level of authority and empowerment so that they can influence all areas of IT in order to achieve the process goal.
- It is important to ensure that the right resources are in place with the required skills and competencies and the right technology to support the process.
- There may be difficulty in understanding the value of Capacity Management so it is important to communicate that value, consistently from the top down.
- If current levels of capacity are considered 'good', there may be no business justification to deploy the process.
- It is important not to define too large a scope for Capacity Management or total gridlock may result.

CHAPTER 12 Service Level Management

The journey of Service Level Management (SLM) involves negotiating, defining, managing and improving the quality of IT services at an acceptable cost to the business. The journey occurs in an environment of rapidly changing business requirements, increased demands and cost pressure. To optimize this journey, the IT organization needs to strike the right balance between business expectations and what IT can actually deliver. To that end, the journey of Service Level Management process line (figure 12.1) is an exercise in managing simple IT economics, customer perceptions and building business relationships. This often involves organizational and cultural change, since the IT organization needs to move from 'systems' to 'services based thinking. A major benefit of SLM is that it enables overall IT service performance to be measured, managed and reported on.

From an ITIL perspective, effective SLM results in a sound working relationship between IT and the business. Along this critical journey, IT and the business forge SLAs or contracts. These agreements document IT services that are designed to meet Service Level Requirements (SLRs) and agreed service targets, and should never force either IT or the business do something that is unacceptable. Service Level Management should be a means to building partnerships and working collaboratively toward the same common goal.

Many organizations, unfortunately, use service contracts to convey service delivery in terms that are not relevant or meaningful to the business, and often increase conflict. IT must realize that SLM is a journey for both IT and its customers— one of partnership and collaboration that helps IT and the business to forge a stronger relationship based on common organizational business goals and objectives.

In SLM, ITIL places great emphasis on a Service Catalog, which is comprised of IT services to which an end user can subscribe, along with standard service levels and associated costs. A Service Catalog is one of the most important elements of SLM, since it helps IT present itself as a true service provider rather than a technology department. To be truly effective, a Service Catalog presents service levels and costs for each service, and provides a description of the services in the customers own language. The Service Catalog should reflect business processes rather than technology platforms, and must shield the end user from complexities, utilizing automated workflow to complete service activations and fulfillment procedures.

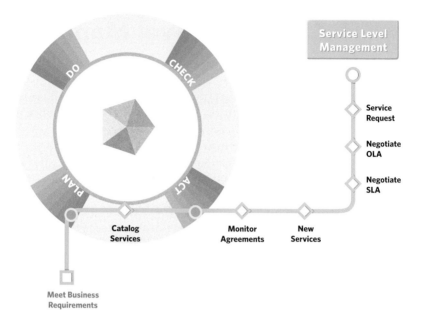

Figure 12.1 Service Level Management Process Line

SERVICE REQUEST

The first stop on the Service Level Management journey is the Service Request station (see figure 12.1). Traditionally, requests for new IT services have been met when IT scrambles to meet every demand. In these situations, every new service request is treated as important, since they have not been prioritized, and IT often lacks the means to assess reliably whether resources are available to meet the demand.

An effective SLM journey starts with IT and the business prioritizing services, and the appropriate service levels required by the business. Technology can play a key role here, centralizing and co-ordinating all service requests, and utilizing portfolio management techniques to prioritize service requests according to agreed business criteria. The Service Request station is critical since it involves uniting IT and the business, and is the foundation upon which agreements are made. At this station, it is essential that IT does not get bogged down in technical details, but works collaboratively with all stakeholders to discuss business needs and requirements. Only when it has achieved this primary goal, can the SLM journey continue to the process of translating the requirements into technical specifications and supporting activities.

NEGOTIATE OLAs

Once services have been identified and prioritized, the process of negotiating agreements between internal IT departments (via Operational Level Agreements - OLAs) and external providers (via Underpinning Contracts) begins. Here, IT begins an internal process of detailing agreements about the delivery of specific elements of an IT service. Every IT service will be underpinned by OLAs, and IT needs a process whereby each element of IT supporting the overall IT service is not only documented, but can be measured, monitored and improved according to how it supports the overall IT service. Defining, drafting and negotiating OLAs is required in order to document the relationship and expectations between the different IT teams, and when performed effectively can help break down 'IT silos' and communication barriers.

Creating and using OLAs is an iterative process. Business requirements and technology are constantly changing, which may alter any IT capabilities. For these reasons, the process involves continuously matching IT capabilities to changing business requirements, and periodically reassessing existing OLAs. This requires discussion and agreement between IT departments. Technology can help by establishing automatic links between OLAs and Underpinning Contracts, with automatic alerts sent to the Service Level Manager when values do not match.

NEGOTIATE SLAs

An SLA is a formal agreement between the customer(s) and the IT service provider specifying service levels and the terms under which a service or a package of services is provided to the customer. Remember, SLAs are used for internal customers. If IT and the customer do not work collaboratively, true service quality improvements will not happen. Both parties must agree on the goals. This is achieved by setting up meetings with the customer to commence negotiations on the structure of the SLAs, and the levels of service to be provided. The objective is to match the customer's expectation with what can be achieved, negotiating a 'win-win' situation for both parties. Here begins the drafting and definition of SLAs to mirror the formal agreements from the negotiation meeting. This is the basis of an SLA or contract.

The service achievements have to meet the agreed targets, and therefore service levels have to be monitored with appropriate tools. This should be done from a customer's perspective. It is important to note that Service Level Management involves continually checking to make sure there is improvement, which is why it is made up of iterative process activities. As with OLA negotiation, technology can also help optimize the SLA negotiation process activity, including, but not limited to, automation of customizable templates, ability to track and display SLA audit change logs, provide links to the values in related OLAs and underpinning contracts with notification when values do not correlate.

Now that IT services have been defined, and OLAs and SLAs drafted and signed off, it is time to address the next process activity (or the next 'station' on the SLM journey).

> ### NEW
> ### SERVICES

At this point, new services that are introduced in the environment should be communicated to all Customers who may use these services. This means that the Service Level Requirements (SLRs) of the service are achievable, and that the SLAs of existing services will not be impacted because of poor planning. These new services and their associated requirements are now documented in contract form.

> ### MONITOR
> ### AGREEMENTS

As we move to the Monitor Agreements station, we are armed with documented service requirements, service level targets and negotiated agreements. To optimize service quality, the monitoring and audit of SLAs must be captured in meaningful reports and performed on a periodic basis. These reports should highlight key metrics that indicate areas of improvement and gaps between capabilities and agreed upon service levels. At this stage of the journey, it is important to identify what metrics are meaningful to the business, establish goals for a sound baseline, review the results against that baseline, and be able to coach and measure staff on their performance in achieving service levels - taking corrective action to avoid service degradations and service level breaches. Technology can support monitoring of service levels and should be able to integrate with system management software to alert Service Level Managers automatically when SLAs are going to be breached.

CATALOG SERVICES

As we approach the end of the SLM process we arrive at the Catalog Services station. A Service Catalog identifies and documents all IT services. It specifies key IT service features, options and service levels, and is a non-technical document using common terms of reference. Eventually the Service Catalog will become a master SLA, describing every IT service, SLA and supporting OLAs in the customers own language. The Service Catalog is a vital communications tool, helping IT profile itself as a true service provider more able to manage customer demand and expectations.

Technology and process automation can greatly help here, by enabling the IT organization quickly to build and present an online catalog of business facing IT services. These IT services are presented in terms understandable by the business, and ideally provide workflow to ensure the services are quickly provisioned, together with automated monitoring of the underlying service levels.

On the administrative side, security technology can ensure that controls are in place to allow only authorized personnel to view, create and alter the Service Catalog, SLAs, OLAs and underpinning contracts. Integration with Change Management is also supported by technology through the automatic ability to track and display detailed audit logs recording changes to the Service Catalog.

MEET BUSINESS REQUIREMENTS

As we approach the end of the Service Level Management process, optimization and automation of many process activities will have helped build a service-centric culture and closer relationship with the business. As with all ITIL processes, Service Level Management is a journey of continuous improvement, with the focus here on continuously reviewing the business validity of underpinning contracts, OLAs and SLAs against the Service Catalog. Regular meetings will be undertaken to ensure service contracts are still current and relevant to the organization; this is the foundation of continuous service improvement and the goal of Service Level Management to meet business objectives. This is an ongoing continuous service improvement process; as new changes are introduced to the environment, there is a cycle of defining, agreeing and negotiating, and a check and balance to ensure alignment with the business.

To ensure meeting business requirements, both business and IT stakeholders should participate in service review meetings, discussing trends on service performance, assigning ownership for incidents causing defects, and working together to remediate defects and continuously measure the impact of changes. A formal plan is then documented and put in place to carry out this remediation, the Service Improvement Plan (SIP).

12.1 Optimizing the Service Level Management Journey

To be truly optimized, Service Level Management needs to integrate with other Service Delivery processes and many Service Support processes too. For example, IT services are made up CIs that define the relationships between CI, people and processes that make up the IT services offered through the Service Catalog, and form the foundation for SLA, OLA and underpinning contract development, negotiation and monitoring.

With such an all-encompassing critical process, process automation is vital, and it should deliver the following capabilities:

- monitoring of service levels and notification of service level thresholds and breaches that provide automatic alerts based on the SLA, business rules and escalation procedures
- the ability to build and measure OLAs and aggregate to SLAs and contracts
- a controlled secure means of access
- Web-enabled client access offering integration with other applications and the CMDB
- integration across both Service Support and Service Delivery processes
- ability to build and present an online actionable and fully integrated Service Catalog

12.2 Avoiding Service Level Management Problems

The following recommendations will help to avoid Service Level Management Problems:

- Never ignore the integration points to all of the other ITIL processes. As each process is being designed, it is important to recognize that there are key touch-points between all of the processes. It is vital to understand that there is a certain level of integration (inputs become outputs) that naturally takes place.
- Do not define IT services without collaborating with the business (the customer). Do not define and set service targets without customer input, because they must be well understood and agreed upon by both parties in order to avoid any confusion.

- Do not forget that SLAs should be used as a basis for financial allocation/charging and this helps to demonstrate the value that the business is receiving for money spent on IT.
- Without an appointed Service Level Manager, there is no one to ensure compliance and no one is held accountable for the end-to-end process.
- Automation of service level monitoring and breach notification enhances the Service Level Management journey and allows for integration; just be sure to design the process before attempting to automate it.

Service Level Management ensures that all operational and tactical processes (across both Service Support and Service Delivery) are aligned with business needs. Service Level Management has responsibility for the customer perception of the IT organization, and is the only ITIL process that involves direct negotiation with customers.

Process automation can help optimize SLA by providing an online list of all customer facing IT services (via a Service Catalog), and by building, measuring and reporting on SLAs from an end-user perspective.

CHAPTER 13 Financial Management for IT Services

The goal of Financial Management for IT Services is to ensure that IT expenditure is managed to allow IT to deliver exactly the services that best support the business goals of the organization in the most cost effective manner. Financial Management will oversee the allocation of IT expenditure to services and manage the recovery of the costs of those services from the business customers to whom they are provided. Financial Management encompasses the activities which establish the expenditure expectations of the organization, the tracking of how costs are accrued and money is spent, the management of financial assets, and the association of these costs against the various service consumers within the organization. ITIL recognizes that different types of service organizations have different needs in terms of granularity and precision of financial management information. However, with the sizeable investments that most enterprises make in IT, evidence of sound governance and fiscal management practices are increasingly necessary for compliance and external regulatory purposes.

Financial Management must address two key questions:

Firstly, 'Are we doing the right things?' Do we invest in the right projects? Are the services that we provide exactly what the business needs, in terms of functionality, availability, cost and quality? What value does IT deliver to the business?

Secondly, 'Are we doing things right?' Are we delivering IT services as cost efficiently as possible? Where can we improve? Should we do things ourselves or can someone else provide the service more efficiently?

It can be argued that the Financial Management subway line (figure 13.1) underpins all of the other ITIL Service Delivery tracks. Availability, capacity and IT service continuity plans are generated to ensure that the organization's service levels are achieved and they are drafted in line with the available budget that the organization holds. Financial Management therefore acts as a 'check and balance' to ensure that all service management practices are cost effective and align with business objectives.

Budgeting, IT Accounting and Charging activities (or 'cost allocation' if chargeback is seen as counter-cultural or infeasible to an organization) rely upon the establishment of a cost model for all IT expenditure. Subsequent reconciling activities, usage analysis and cost metrics are measured against this model. The role of technology, therefore, is to ensure that the cost model can be held in some electronic form, to measure usage, expenditure and activity automatically, to aggregate and reconcile these measurements and, finally, to allocate costs - adjusted for service quality or service consumption volumes back to cost centers or other organizational structures.

Let us examine now how technology can be applied to optimize each stage (see figure 13.1) of the journey from the initial planning of Financial Management for IT Services and the process terminus of that journey - the efficient and cost-effective stewardship of IT assets and resources and management of IT Investments.

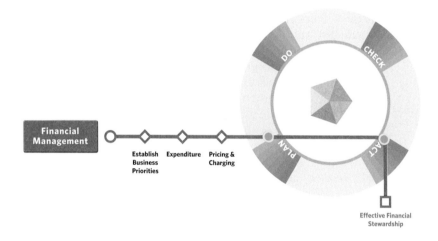

Figure 13.1 Financial Management for IT Services Process Line

The journey begins with planning the policies, objectives, activities, disciplines and resources required for the appropriate Financial Management controls. At this stage, technology evaluation typically touches on existing company financial and accounting systems, and project management tools. Almost any organization will have accounting practices in place and can easily report the cost of hardware, software, employment, accommodation or external services. But how are these resources used by the organization? Can we benchmark the cost of IT services for a business process? Even if there is no intention of charging IT costs back to the business organization, there is a growing need to gain more transparency about the cost of service and resource utilization.

Existing accounting systems and practices need to be extended and one must consider how existing operational monitoring tools, inventory tools and service level assurance technology could be exploited to provide accounting and usage information. Thought should also be given to how the financial information is to be delivered to the business and other interested parties, who may need to consider portal and role-oriented dashboard capabilities. The cost model may need to be representative of the goods and services offered in the IT Service Catalog, hence technology may need to be considered in parallel with Service Level Management requirements.

ESTABLISH BUSINESS PRIORITIES

Our first stop is to establish how IT investments should be prioritized and how the IT budget should be allocated. By its very nature, much of the IT infrastructure and organization will support business processes of varying or conflicting priorities. Therefore, a key technology deliverable is to enable the comparison of various IT activities and projects in multiple business-context dimensions, such as cost, efficiency, customer satisfaction, quality, growth, compliance and other corporate goals, such that IT organizations can arrive at an optimized portfolio of projects and operational activities in line with business priorities, whilst balanced against the resources and budget available to IT.

The IT Service Continuity line also arrives at this station, since this process has similar reliance on establishing business priorities in terms of the vital business functions and the critical business processes which support them. All organizations need to ensure that sufficient investment is made to reduce operational risks and to operate the business continuity plans as they relate to IT activity. This again relies on accurate project and portfolio controls, but also has a critical reliance upon accurate inventory and related technologies – which are similarly essential in establishing an accurate cost basis for financial management.

EXPENDITURE

Having established the relative priorities of IT activities in line with business objectives, operational practices lead naturally to expenditure and cost accrual. The cost model and charging policies will dictate the granularity to which expenditure needs to be tracked. However, in procuring IT hardware and software assets, good governance relies upon the operational view of these assets (typically focused on inventory, availability and performance) being synchronized with the service, financial and contractual views - thus ensuring that the right resources are cost effectively deployed for the right business purposes.

Integrated IT Asset Management technology plays an important role here, and is similarly important to identification and verification stages in Configuration Management. Technology integration is an important consideration as separate business systems will track other costs, and this information may need to be aggregated with resource (people) costs, and with hardware and software costs to deliver a complete view of expenditure. The ability to influence expenditure based on prior knowledge of the costs will also require service catalog technology which aggregates direct and indirect costs as part of the IT service description.

Many passengers on this journey feel that the pricing and charging station is the most congested and sometimes the most difficult, and some even decide to avoid it altogether. As the business naturally needs to bear the cost of IT services, issues surround the model for how the costs should be recovered, who should pay and how value for money should be measured. While it might be simpler for IT to be a 'utility' cost to the business, equally shared by all, this model might skew the internal balance sheet of individual lines of business with important political consequences.

Similarly, directly charging a line of business for only the activities conducted on its behalf and the proportion of infrastructure it uses requires a granular level of accounting which may not be cost justified in terms of the benefits gained by the extra accuracy. Certainly, charges should be related to business transactions or activities. Reports on CPU seconds and network bandwidth utilization do not necessarily help the business users to understand and optimize their cost (although these are important metrics on the capacity line).

In order to provide the transparency required, prices for services must be related to a well defined catalog of business oriented IT services. A further dimension is that the price of services might be dependent on the quality of service actually delivered. The technology challenge is to associate the IT budget with the IT services offered and the IT assets used to arrive at an overall service cost, and then associate IT activities, utilization and the quality of IT services with the consumers of these services in order to arrive at an allocation of these costs. Ideally, there should be integration with the Service Catalog technology, the service level metering and availability monitoring technology, and the asset inventory with aggregated costs, with the ability to reconcile these to the budgetary components to feed service billing technology.

En-route to our next stop, we come to another intersection, which illustrates the difficulty in ensuring the right levels of investment are managed in order to meet current and new business requirements whilst maintaining service levels and mitigating risks. Under-investing in any of these areas can have serious implications for all of the business; hence, technology can be leveraged to enable the IT portfolio to be optimized which is essential to business success.

13.1 Optimizing the Financial Management Journey

The underlying goal of Financial Management for IT Services is for IT assets and resources to be obtained, deployed, utilized, changed and disposed of cost effectively. In many organizations, there will already be technology involved in the operational aspect of these stages, but this is unlikely to extend to cover the financial management aspects. To enhance the Financial Management process, technology must therefore provide:

- a view of the current book value of IT assets for use in cross charge or cost allocation activity
- a view of the total cost of IT assets across their entire life cycle
- integration with contract and license repositories in order to accommodate vendor management activity within financial management
- an ability to automate the allocation of costs for a service to a business unit or user at the point of request for that service (i.e. an inherent part of the provisioning process)
- an ability to reconcile service charges with service quality to ensure that these are in balance as far as the business is concerned
- accommodation of flexible charging structures such as flat rate, usage based, tiered or quality-based
- the ability to take existing operational data sources to provide details of utilization and IT service quality
- the ability to associate the elements of the cost model with the elements in the budget, with the elements in the IT service catalog that provide consistent constructs for both IT and the business

Finally, we arrive at our destination - a point at which the planned budget of IT expenditure is fully accounted for by the scheduled and unscheduled deployment of IT resources and infrastructure, and where these deployment decisions are evidently cost effective and aligned with business priorities. As a result, the business is able to see the value it receives from IT, and can trust that the IT organization is run under fiscal controls consistent with other business functions. It can see that the service levels delivered by IT are relevant to the costs of that service. Therefore, it is simply not enough to have well managed investments, it is equally important to demonstrate that this is the case. Technology's role is to provide the automated information collection and aggregation used for service and customer-level cost allocation and service level assurance. Technology must hold and assist the creation of the IT service cost model, and it must provide reporting and visualization for both business managers and IT managers alike.

13.2 Avoiding Financial Management Problems

- **Perception and Reality.** Apart from fiscal diligence, one of the functions of Financial Management is to provide evidence that IT activities and costs are aligned to business priorities. IT loses credibility and business partnership if the basis of charging is not 'fairly' distributed. Hence any service charges must also show the direct and indirect breakdown of charges.
- **Empowerment.** What decisions can the business now make on the basis of 'transparent' IT cost / charge information? For example, can it control its own cost base? Can it change how and when it uses the services? If the opportunity to change behavior is limited, the cost effectiveness of establishing complex charging and billing systems may be questionable.
- **Integration.** By linking the service catalogue to the budget and automating service provision, this can dramatically simplify the activities for Financial Management, and can also feed into Service Level Management automation.
- **Cost transparency** and especially charge back of IT cost will change the behaviors of users and customers. It must be planned (and adjusted) carefully in order to avoid undesired results (eg inadequate pricing may lead to over utilization of external resources over existing internal resources).
- **Lack of conceptual work** when implementing charge back in large client server environments risks heavy congestions due to diversity of information and velocity of change. Automating the collection and mediation of metrics is essential to avoid the benefits of chargeback being outweighed by the costs.

CHAPTER 14 Service Continuity Management

The main objective of ITSCM is to support the overall business continuity management process by ensuring that the required IT technical and service facilities can be recovered within required and agreed business timescales.

Disasters do not happen every day, but planning, is an ongoing event. The IT organization needs to build and maintain plans that effectively respond to major business disruptions.

As you see from figure 14.1, the process activities (or stations) on the ITSCM journey include:

- assess the risks to IT service continuity and the impact that any disruption to service may have on the business
- identify critical business services and ensure that preventative measures are applied based on potential risks and severity of impact
- determine a work breakdown structure that ensures that services are restored within the timeframes required by the business
- manage risk by implementing mitigation and contingency plans
- define the desired approach to restore service
- develop and test recovery plans and maintain a master recovery plan

ITIL identifies two specific aspects to continuity management:
- **Business Continuity Management** is responsible for planning business recovery from disaster. It creates and implements the master recovery plan that the entire business follows. Each organization within the business may have requirements for specific recovery planning that is unique to it.
- **IT Service Continuity Management** is responsible for restoring IT services in response to disasters in support of the business continuity management plan.

The first station (often called the initiation stage) of ITSCM is involved with defining the scope of the process. ITSCM is dependent on how well the business as a whole implements business continuity management. There is a natural limit to how much ITSCM can accomplish in an environment where little or no business continuity management is conducted. ITSCM should make every effort to ensure that its activities are supported and budgeted at the highest levels in conjunction with an active business continuity effort. Initiating continuity management is often a major organizational change and requires significant diplomatic skill, executive buy-in, and organizational agility.

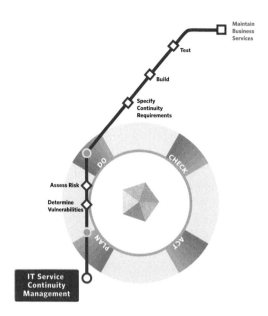

Figure 14.1 IT Service Continuity Management Subway Line

Imagine attempting to think about these activities in isolation from the other ITIL processes. Even positioning this process in the Service Delivery cycle (as it is in the ITIL book) is not going to help you holistically to plan for disaster recovery. The Plan-Do-Check-Act continuous improvement cycle allows you to incrementally improve the plans you need to have in place across both the Service Delivery and Service Support processes that all support IT Service Continuity. For example, when planning ITSCM think about whether or not you are aware of all infrastructure changes that could affect recovery plans, or whether you can easily baseline and reproduce configurations needed to fully restore IT services.

The initiation of the ITSCM process affects the entire IT organization and is where the following activities are conducted:

- **Policy Setting.** The policy should be defined as quickly as possible and communicated across the organization. This activity determines the boundaries within which continuity management will operate.
- **Specify Terms of Reference and Scope** is the activity of defining roles and areas of responsibility within continuity management.
- **Allocate Resources** is the activity of ensuring that sufficient resources are in place to support the goals of continuity management.
- **Define the Project Organization and Control Structure** is the activity of applying structured project management methodologies to continuity management.

- **Agree on Project and Quality Plans** is the activity of obtaining buy-in and active participation of all individuals and groups within the organization.

These are all planning processes, but they lead to actions that execute the plans and, of course, to the review of the actions and their success.

DETERMINE VULNERABILITY

The next station on the ITSCM journey really provides the foundation for ITSCM. Structures that typically survive disasters only survive if their foundations are well constructed and vulnerability has been analyzed. Organizations are no different. Furthermore, the strength of the foundation significantly impacts the costs that will be incurred by the recovery effort.

ASSESS RISK

Risk Assessment is the second key driver in determining ITSCM requirements. It involves the likelihood of any given disastrous event occurring and the level of service disruption that is likely to result. The science of risk assessment is supported by many risk analysis methodologies resulting from consistently applied statistical principles. CRAMM (CCTA Risk Analysis and Management Method) is the risk assessment methodology endorsed by ITIL.

SPECIFY CONTINUITY REQUIREMENTS

This stage involves building requirements and developing a specific strategy that determines risk prevention measures and recovery options. It can be organized into two sections: ITSCM Requirements and Strategy.

14.1 ITSCM Requirements

Business Impact Analysis is the first key driver in determining ITSCM requirements and involves identifying potential losses that a company is likely to endure if a disaster occurs. To do a business impact analysis effectively, the organization must identify all of the critical business processes and their dependent IT services, and the potential business impacts of IT service disruption. This information is the basis for costing ITSCM projects and for recovery planning. It is also one of the key areas where you need to 'visit' the service support processes to establish baselines of IT configurations that need to be restored following disasters, and to ensure the currency and accuracy of ITSCM plans through established change procedures.

The business impact analysis also identifies:

- the form that the damage or loss may take, including lost income, additional costs, damaged reputation, loss of goodwill, and loss of competitive advantage
- how the degree of damage or loss is likely to escalate after a service disruption
- the staffing, skills, facilities, and services (including the IT services) necessary to enable critical and essential business processes to continue operating at a minimum acceptable level
- the time within which minimum levels of staffing, facilities, and services should be recovered
- the time within which all required business processes and supporting staff, facilities, and services should be fully recovered

Business services will then be ranked based on their importance to the business and the need to have them restored rapidly. Those with the greatest need are restored first, which requires first restoring the critical sub-services that support each business service.

Impacts are measured against particular scenarios for each business process (eg order to cash), such as an inability to process orders or to send invoices to customers. Impacts typically fall into one or more of the following categories:

- failure to achieve agreed upon internal service levels
- financial loss
- additional costs
- immediate and long-term loss of market share
- breach of law, regulations, or standards
- risk to personal safety
- political, corporate, or personal embarrassment
- breach of moral responsibility
- loss of goodwill

- loss of credibility
- loss of image and reputation
- loss of operational capability, for example, in a command and control environment

14.2 Strategy

The information collected during the requirements and risk assessment phase is used to determine an appropriate ITSCM strategy that incorporates the right balance between risk reduction measures (mitigation) and recovery planning (contingency).

Mitigation means reducing the likelihood that an event will occur or that it will disrupt service if it does occur. Typical mitigation or risk reduction measures include:

- comprehensive back-up and recovery strategy including off-site storage
- eliminating of single points of failure, such as electrical power, access to facilities, etc.
- outsourcing services to more than one supplier
- building resilient IT systems
- improving security controls

This measure is just as important for service support processes. These actions have consequences that need to be reviewed and, if necessary, altered to reflect holistic planning.

Contingency involves recovering from an event when it does happen. Contingency or recovery plans need to be prepared for:

- staff and accommodation
- IT systems and networks
- critical services, such as power, communications, water
- critical assets, such as paper records and reference materials

There are six recovery options that an organization can choose from when implementing contingency plans:

1. **Do nothing is an approach that no** businesses can afford, but in some cases the organization has determined that recovery is too expensive and that no recovery attempts will be made.
2. **Manual (Paper Based) Workarounds,** in some cases a minor or less important service can be provided manually.
3. **Reciprocal Arrangements** were typically seen in the mainframe era. Companies would make arrangements with other companies to provide access to computer equipment for an agreed period if the other company experienced a disaster.

4. **Gradual Recovery,** often called 'Cold Standby', provides a recovery site that is an empty shell with a minimum of basic services including cabling, air-conditioning, etc.
5. **Intermediate Recovery,** often called 'Warm Standby', requires a recovery site with all basic services and configured hardware.
6. **Immediate Recovery** is often called 'Hot Standby'.

Some of these recovery facilities come in several variations that are a combination of four basic types:

- **Dedicated facilities** are those facilities that are reserved for use by one specific company and can either be owned by the company or leased from a third party.
- **Non-dedicated facilities** are those facilities that may be shared by two or more companies. They work on the principle that most disasters are localized. This principle allows a facilities provider to have a small number of facilities supporting a larger number of companies. In normal circumstances, only a few companies experience disasters at any one time, and adequate facilities exist to support their needs.
- **These types of facilities** are excellent for localized disasters, but inadequate for large scale disasters affecting many companies. The primary reason these sites are utilized is that they cost less than dedicated sites.
- **Fixed facilities** are those facilities housed in buildings that cannot be moved.
- **Portable facilities** are those facilities housed in portable buildings that can be positioned in multiple locations depending on need.

The Build station of the ITSCM journey includes the following five activities:

- organization and implementation planning
- implementing stand by arrangements
- developing recovery plans
- implementing risk reduction measures
- developing procedures

Organization and Implementation Planning. Planning, testing and practicing will enable the business to recover quickly and may mean the difference between survival and going out of business. The 'practicing' allows for continuous improvement and, of course, allows lessons to be learned from actually conducting or 'doing' the process that may lead to changes to many activities.

There are three tiers of recovery effort that need to be identified in organizational planning:

- **executive** - which has the overall authority and control for all recovery efforts
- **co-ordination** - which is responsible for co-ordinating the overall recovery effort within the organization
- **recovery** - which includes the individuals and teams responsible for implementing the actual recovery plans

There are three levels of planning that need to be considered overall:

- co-ordination planning
- key support function planning
- recovery team planning

Co-ordinated planning includes the development of the following formal plans:

- emergency response plan
- damage assessment plan
- salvage plan
- vital records plan
- crisis management and public relations plan

Particularly after a test of the activities, it is vital to update these plans with any lessons learned in order to maintain their usefulness. Support function planning includes the following formal plans:

- accommodation and services plan
- computer systems and network plan
- telecommunication plan
- security plan
- personnel plan
- finance and administration plan

Implement Standby Arrangements. Recovery from disaster requires that standby arrangements exist and can be implemented. They include providing standby facilities and equipment, as well as building standby infrastructure and managing contracts with third party suppliers. These arrangements are the contingency options chosen in requirements and strategy phase (discussed above). While at this station, plans for implementing these options are created.

Develop Recovery Plans. The recovery plans and the proof that they can be effectively executed are the deliverables of continuity management short of a disaster actually occurring. Therefore, developing the plans is the major activity of ITSCM.

Implement Risk Reduction Measures. This phase is when the prevention or risk mitigation options discussed above are actually implemented. Typical risk reduction measures include:

- provision of UPS capabilities
- the development of fault tolerant systems
- offsite storage and archiving
- duplication of data storage

Develop Procedures. It may often be necessary to have technical people, who are unfamiliar with system recovery. For this reason, detailed procedures should be in place and available when needed.

The Test station (often called the implementation stage) of the ITSCM journey includes the testing activity:

- initial testing

Initial Testing. Testing is a critical element of the overall ITSCM process and is the only way of ensuring that the selected strategy, stand-by arrangements, logistics, business recovery plans and procedures will work in practice. Tests should be performed initially after a plan is developed, and then following any major changes.

The Maintain Business Services station is the final stage on the ITSCM journey. It includes those operational activities that keep service continuity plans active and current. IT environments are in a constant state of change, which causes Continuity Management plans to become outdated quickly. This condition necessitates that many activities taking place in the service support processes (e.g. Configuration Management) subway line need to be coordinated with the ITSCM subway line and vice versa. Resources need to be applied to ensure that the plans reflect the current state of the organization at all times. Therefore, Continuity Management needs to be a part of every change decision.

This stage of the process should include the following activities:

- **Testing** - recovery plans should be tested on an ongoing basis to ensure that they perform as required, and to determine additional weaknesses
- **Training and Awareness** - effective training and organizational awareness of ITSCM is critical to ensuring success of the process
- **Review** - to ensure that all aspects of the plans are complete and up-to-date
- **Change Control** - Change Management plays an important role in keeping all plans current, and in determining the impact of any infrastructure changes to the recovery plan
- **Assurance** - obtaining assurance that ITSCM is adequate to meet the business needs of the organization

14.3 Optimizing the IT Service Continuity Management Journey

Although ITSCM differs from Availability Management in that Continuity Management is responsible for large-scale loss of services due to a disastrous event and Availability Management is responsible for the day-to-day provision of service availability, it is clear that ITIL process separation involved a good deal of hair-splitting that may not be reflected in the real world where functions are often combined, or indeed neglected. A practical approach is to use our ITIL subway process map to think about the major areas of overlap and also the interfaces where plans need to be all-embracing.

There are no substitutes for brainstorming in the ITSCM process, and it is unrealistic to attempt to automate many of the planning activities. A full understanding of where the key intersections are for all of the Service Support and Delivery processes, and how each process must be considered within the ITSCM plan, is needed. And that understanding must be formed with the specific requirements of your business in mind.

Planning for ITSCM is similar in many ways to planning for capacity or availability; the processes are in themselves supported by the Service Support subway lines but must be planned (and improved) demonstrably in line with the needs of the business rather than with IT goals. Many organizations make the elementary mistake of planning for disasters in relation to IT without thinking of business issues (believing that both will have the same goals). Many more simply pay lip service by building a generic plan that is inadequate. It is a high risk strategy to plan ITSCM without a full understanding of its impact across all ITlL processes.

APPENDIX A Apollo 13: Learning from Simulations to help ensure business success

> 'If we didn't have the knowledge gained in Simulation training the Astronauts of Apollo 13 would not be here today.'
> - Gene Kranz, Flight Controller Apollo 13.

A.1 Introduction

In the aerospace industry, simulations are a critical component of competence development. Simulations serve to test knowledge, skills and behavior of the crews and Mission Operations Control staff. They also help ensure that everybody understands and can fulfill their tasks, roles and responsibilities, and can follow standard, agreed upon practices and procedures. Simulations help to identify deficiencies and prioritize improvement needs in both the processes and the competence development, to ensure success in the live mission situation. This is exactly what is required of staff adopting ITSM best practices such as the ITIL. We can learn from NASA and use simulations to help ensure that people understand, apply and continually improve ITSM best practices in order to realize business success.

ITIL business simulation training can help and enable your IT organization:

- understand how IT performance impacts the business
- improve its capability in managing IT in relation to business needs
- reduce the risk of your ITIL or ITSM initiatives going wrong
- increase the buy in and commitment to ITIL and ITSM best practices at all levels within your organization
- recognize and learn how to use ITIL to realize measurable performance gains and add value to the business, and at the same time reduce business risk
- learn to work as a team instead of individuals in organizational silos
- identify and capture improvement needs within your own organization

To do this, we must examine:

- the current challenges facing CIOs that drive the need for ITSM best practices
- common approaches and mistakes in adopting and deploying ITIL
- what is a simulation and why they are necessary

- how the ITIL Business simulation works
- what the simulation delivers in terms of results

The Current Challenges facing CIOs

With the ever increasing use and dependence upon IT to sustain and improve business performance, delivering IT operational excellence is becoming a critical capability for most IT organizations. IT organizations are faced with a need to demonstrate 'control of IT' and at the same time to demonstrate 'performance and added value'.

Control

IT must show that it is in control. It must show that costs can be managed, guarantee security and integrity of business information, guarantee availability and continuity of business operations, demonstrate that it can protect assets and reduce business risks associated with IT. Increasing pressure from legislative controls such as Sarbanes Oxley, demand this level of 'compliance & control'.

Performance

IT must show that it can perform as required and as agreed with the business. IT must show how it can rapidly and reliably deploy new IT solutions, maintain and improve quality of IT services to the business users, and realize customer satisfaction. IT must be able to demonstrate the 'business value' of IT investments, including investments in ITSM projects.

In the words of Gene Kranz the Apollo 13 Flight director, 'Failure is not an option …' Outsourcing, however, is. IT organizations that fail to demonstrate 'Control' and 'Performance' capabilities will pose an unacceptable risk to business operations and will prevent the business from realizing performance improvement and value through its IT investments. As an IT manager responsible for your organizations IT you must ask yourself three questions:

- Do we deliver operational excellence?
- What must we do as our business grows and becomes more dependent upon IT?
- Is our approach acceptable to the business?

A.2 Common approaches and mistakes in adopting/deploying ITIL

The reality of the last 10 years, certainly in Europe, has been that the anticipated service improvements to be realized by ITIL have been, in reality, difficult to achieve.

ITIL has been seen and described as too bureaucratic and inflexible. The fact is, these failures have little to do with ITIL. It is the way in which ITIL is adopted and deployed that is the problem.

Why is this? People are generally the biggest barrier to achieving sustained results.

Adopting ITIL and buying enabling tools is doomed to failure if the 'people issues' are not addressed. This means more than simply sending staff on training courses and getting them trained in ITIL. It is necessary that people:

- buy into and accept the fact that they need to change the way they do things
- realize the benefits of ITIL to their own work and to the business
- understand what it takes to adopt and deploy ITIL processes
- are committed to making it happen, *and* making it work

'People' includes IT staff at all levels from the CIO down to the operational layers, and indeed also the business and the users. Adopting ITIL is to agree to embark on a journey of organizational change, changing the way people behave. ITIL is the goal.

Another common mistake made is that instead of adopting and applying ITIL to solve a problem or to realize some measurable benefits, ITIL becomes the goal: 'We are going to implement ITIL, because everybody else is doing it'.

Key reasons why adopting ITIL fails to deliver real results or real value:

- lack of insight into the real pain areas that need resolving
- lack of prioritization of improvement initiatives; which initiatives will relieve pain and deliver the most tangible results?
- unclear goals of improvement initiatives: 'when is this initiative considered a success?'
- inability to measure and demonstrate success
- lack of communication, effective two-way communication; communication about the improvement initiative; about 'what it is going to mean'; about 'how we now need to work'; about managing all stakeholder expectations, including the business
- lack of a shared perception over the real need, the real aim and the consequences if improvements are not realized
- lack of involvement and active participation by those who need to improve
- procedures become the goal themselves and are not seen as an agreement between two parties, with inputs, outputs, tasks, roles, responsibilities and dependencies defined and accepted

- no real commitment at all levels; there being a difference between commitment and involvement
- lack of ownership for the improvements, coupled with a lack of leadership; leading, motivating and embedding change
- the implementation is characterized by Plan, Do, Stop, Blame; a one time, massive implementation project effort, instead of a continual process of on-going improvement

A business simulation will get people from all departments to work together as a team to recognize, discuss and agree the pain that needs resolving with ITIL and the goals to be realized.

Buy software immediately

The phrase 'A fool with a tool is still a fool' sums up another misguided approach, commonly made by highly technology focused companies. The approach is: 'We need ITIL. Which tool shall we buy?' When ITIL was first published on CD-ROM, it was not uncommon to find that, after purchasing the CD, a follow-up call asked 'How do I install ITIL in my company ... we want to start working with the ITIL tool.' This type of company thinks that a tool will solve all their problems. Although a tool is vital in managing today's complex IT environments, a tool alone will not solve the issues.

A.3 Where does ITIL go wrong and what can you do about it?

Traditionally, after making a decision to adopt ITIL, IT organizations send their staff on ITIL courses, such as the ITIL Foundations and ITIL Service manager training, assuming that this will give staff the knowledge necessary for effectively deploying ITIL best practices, and hoping that the training will help gain buy in and commitment. The principal focus of much of this type of traditional classroom training is ITIL theory. This type of training provides a solid basis, a common language, and is supported by examination and certification to ensure that people understand the theory. However, this type of training also provides little help when it comes to the practicalities of change. A characteristic of this level of training is that it imparts large amounts of 'information'. However, information is not 'knowledge'. One definition of knowledge is that 'knowledge' is based upon 'experience'.

A business simulation helps people translate theory into knowledge by experiencing ITIL in action. Further details on the value of business simulation are included at the end of this book.

A.4 What is a business simulation?

In a simulation, participants are placed in an imagined environment. In this environment they act in roles. The way in which participants work together as a team, make agreements and design their own processes and procedures, determines the success or failure of the simulation scenario.

In the simulation they are tested with events and must respond to them using the procedures and agreements, the tasks, roles and responsibilities they have made and agreed. Simulations are often played in a number of rounds, so that after each round the team has a chance to 'assess and measure' their level of performance, and to reflect and identify improvements, so that they can 'continually improve'.

A.5 What are the benefits of a simulation?

In a simulation, people can test and apply new theories in a safe environment. People can quickly see the impacts of their decisions and behavior on performance, and can see the impact of changes within the simulated environment. Simulations can be used to learn new skills and to practice new behavior.

Also, people can relate learning discoveries to the real environment, including what have they learnt and what have they applied in the simulation that can be transferred to their real environment.

A.6 What is the Apollo 13 simulation and how does it work?

In this simulation participants are placed in the environment of the Mission Operations Control room of Apollo 13. The simulation re-enacts the Apollo 13 mission and the actual events that occurred. Why choose Apollo 13 as a simulation case? Apollo 13 is an example of a team of specialists supporting mission critical technology and systems. A post mission review revealed that it was integrated people, process and supporting technology that led to success. What has become known as the most successful failure in the history of the space program has also become an example to all support organizations of what 'Operational excellence' means. In the simulation the team must try to recreate the success of Apollo 13 by applying ITSM best practices. The team must see if they have what it takes to be in Mission Control. The characteristics of the simulation are:

- The participants get to play the roles of the Mission Operations Control team. The team has roles such as The Flight Director (IT Manager), Capsule Communicators (Help Desk), Mission Specialists (2nd Line Support), Specialist Support Team (3rd Line Support), as well as some

ITIL process roles such as Incident Manager, Problem Manager, Change Manager, Capacity Manager and Line Manager roles.
- Participants must work together as a team.
- Process Managers must manage the end-to-end process and the relationships with line management.
- The simulation facilitator assumes the roles of Mission Director (Customer) and Crew (End User), and the Supplier (External Hardware, software and services provider).
- The Team must manage their relationship with the Mission Director and the Crew, as well as their external suppliers.
- Participants receive a set of Mission goals SLAs from NASA.
- The simulation consists of four rounds. In each round the team undergoes the following steps:
    - designing or improving their process
    - applying their process
    - assessing and measuring their processes
    - reporting against performance agreements
    - analyzing and agreeing improvements
- Throughout the simulation the team undergoes Deming's Continuous Improvement Cycles of Plan-Do-Check-Act
- At the end of the simulation, the Team gets to reflect on key learning points and identify improvement needs in their own working environment. These can be used as input to their own improvement program.

The four rounds of the simulation represent the lifecycle of an IT solution, ie the lifecycle of: Building, Supporting, Changing and Optimizing.

Round 1 - Building
In Round 1 the Team must Build and configure the Apollo 13 Rocket using a set of Configuration items. In this round the Team experiences ITIL processes such as Configuration Management and Release Management. Trends show that 70% of IT projects are over time, over budget or fail to deliver the right quality. In Round 1 many teams also fail to deliver on time, within budget or the right quality. At the end of the simulation round they get to reflect on the reasons for this and how they could have prevented this happening.

Round 2 - Supporting
In Round 2 the team must implement the support processes for dealing with Crew requests and incidents, and for solving and preventing problems. At the start of this round they are given their Service Level targets by the Mission Director. These Service Level targets are based upon the balanced scorecard and reflect the type of targets many IT companies are faced with achieving.

Plan & Do
The Teams design their processes & procedures using ITIL or their own knowledge and skills, they agree roles and responsibilities, and they design tools for managing their workload.
Apollo 13 lifts off the launch pad. Incidents and events occur; actual events as experienced in 1970. Standard requests for service, incidents and major problems occur. The team must prioritize and manage their workload with an eye on agreed key performance targets.
At the end of the round we reflect on what happened. What went well? What went wrong? What were the consequences on the business? What were the consequences on your own Team and how do people feel?

Typically what happens is:
People feel frustrated; there is chaos and confusion; they feel they have too much work to do; they feel the workload is unrealistic – they cannot possibly handle all the business requests; they are not in control; they have no idea how well they have performed and understand that the business (Mission Director) and the Business Users (Crew) are dissatisfied. Often people recognize similarities to their own environment. The teams understand, feel and experience the impact of poor processes on performance.

Check & Act
We then reflect on people, process and technology to identify if tasks, roles and responsibilities were defined and executed, and if people behaved as agreed. We use assessment tools such as ISO 20000 checklists, CMM assessments or roadmap models such as CA's ITSM process maps to help the teams to measure and assess process maturity and performance. For example, using the visualization of the Incident Management process map it becomes clear that the Team has no 'escalation' mechanism, and the junction where Incident and Problem Management meet are not in place. We identify the 'non compliance' in their processes and how these contributed to poor performance. We also reflect on how well Teams use a form of tooling to help 'monitor & track' and support escalations. The Team then has to design and decide on their own Service Improvement Plan. They have to make choices such as which improvement actions will relieve pain and deliver the most business benefits. They must convince the business how the improvement choices they make will impact overall performance, reduce risk and add value.

Round 3 - Changing
In Round 3 the Team must implement a process for dealing with Changes, as well as support the ongoing operation. If they do not resolve the poor performance of Round 2, they will not be able to manage changes as well. In this round a significant change must be planned, built, tested, accepted and implemented. The Teams must manage priorities of incidents

and changes and resolve resource conflicts. Process Managers and Line Managers must discuss and agree priorities.

Following Round 3 we reflect again and see if their improvements have had any effect.

Typically, if the team really does implement the agreed improvements we see the following:

People feel less frustrated; there is less chaos and they are less stressed; they feel under control and can show they are meeting their Service Level targets; they see the business and the crew are more satisfied and the relationship with the business has improved. They also feel they can manage the workload and often feel they had less work to do. The reality in this round is that they actually had more work to do. But because they were really more effective and efficient, they were able to handle it all.

In terms of demonstrating performance and added value this round generally illustrates that the changes they made, in terms of improving ITIL processes, improving ownership and accountability of roles, and improving their management tools, mean that they were able to meet their KPIs for the business.

Round 4 - Optimization
In Round 4 they must apply processes for being proactive, and for optimizing performance (capacity demands), and for meeting service and cost agreements. In Round 4 they must manage their resources more effectively, to ensure three complex business projects are carried out, as well as ongoing support and maintenance demands. Some teams succeed and some teams fail. But all teams recognize which success or fail factors underpin their results.

Following the four rounds we perform a post mission review. The intent is to relate what we have learnt and what we applied in the simulation to our own working environment.

A simulation game is a powerful learning instrument. However, it is important to know what learning objective you want to achieve by applying it and what type of behavioral change you want to invoke.
Simply playing a simulation without knowing the results required is a waste of time and effort. To get the maximum benefit from your investment (Return-On-Training) it is important that you are aware of the types of learning goals a simulation can achieve and the types of learning objectives your organization wants to realize.

A simulation can be applied to realize a range of different learning objectives for different target groups within an organization. For example a simulation game can be used to:

- learn ITIL theory
- show the effects of process integration and process dependencies
- show how good processes improve performance and bad processes cause failures, high costs, and dissatisfied customers
- teach people how to analyze and improve a process
- show people the importance of an integrated approach of people, process and technology when making improvements
- let people become a process manager and allow them to manage people in a simulated environment
- experience the importance of working together as teams as opposed to individuals in 'silos' (organizational units)
- improve team working within and between departments
- show the measurable effects of improvements in terms of increased performance (within the simulated environment) for example 'we halved the incident resolution time' and 'we lowered costs by 30% by structuring our work and removing failures and wastage'
- show people the effects of 'non compliant' processes and risks these pose to business continuity
- experience how to use ITIL as a continual improvement approach
- teach people how to use process maps and models, to assess and measure their performance
- learn about leadership, how to ensure people are focused on shared goals, and are motivated to work towards common goals
- learn how to give feedback to each other and address people on their individual responsibilities and accountabilities
- identify a list of learning points and improvement needs that are relevant to their own organization

When applied effectively, the effects of simulations can be dramatic. These are just some of the findings of 1000s of participants in simulation games:

- understood the risks and impact to the business caused by poor processes
- recognized the need to actively engage with customers and the users and involve them in improvement initiatives
- felt the need for accurate reporting to gain insight into pain areas and process bottlenecks that needed improving
- recognized the importance of a logging tool for enabling decision-making, and only registering what is needed for managing the workflow and providing reports
- experienced the benefit of the relationship between Incident Management and Problem Management in reducing costs and improving resolution rates and times

- felt the impact of effective and ineffective leadership in ensuring process success
- 'got the message' – bought into the need for both ITIL and the need for managing process improvement initiatives
- understood how to continually improve processes as a team
- felt the need for clear role definitions and the need to be proactive
- felt the pain of poor priority and escalation mechanisms
- became aware of own role in designing improvements and of sticking to agreed procedures
- felt the consequences and frustration of not sticking to agreed practices
- understood process design and improvement approach - it does not need to be so difficult; within a simulation, teams learnt to analyze, prioritize and improve their own process and saw the immediate effects on performance
- operated across boundaries; the Apollo instrument makes people interactive and helps eliminate acting 'in silos'
- felt and understood the need for good team working
- had fun, in a constructive, productive session that helped with team building
- saw the importance of the processes in achieving results
- recognized dependencies between different roles and between different processes
- felt how their own work became less stressful and chaotic when the processes were working properly

These results clearly show how the information became knowledge. Experience and understanding was gained, as well as insight into why their own initiatives were not succeeding.

Participants went on to use their new found knowledge into making sustainable improvements within their own organization.

Customer Quotes:

–"I went back to the office after the Apollo sessions and everyone is talking about how they can use the ITIL concepts on their existing projects. There are Saturn V rockets on every whiteboard. This has mobilized the whole workforce to embrace change and want to change themselves"
– IT Director

APPENDIX B The Role of education in ITIL Implementation

One of the perennial questions asked in our industry is "if ITIL is a best practice, why then do so many implementations fail to meet expectations?"

In this chapter we explore how ineffective understanding of the role and application of education is a significant factor. We will see that best practice content does not necessarily lead to best practice implementations.

For over twenty years, I - and many others - have been repeating the mantra that any successful application of best practices needs to encompass integrated aspects of *people, process and technology*. Obviously, any program that excludes one of these factors is probably doomed to - at best - limited success from the outset. However, even in projects where all three get at least lip service the results have been mixed.

Why?

One reason is the perspective of those in charge of the transformation. Applying a very broad brush we can generally discern two styles of best practices program. The first uses almost entirely in-house talent, the second almost entirely external talent.

The perspective of both is different:

In-House Talent		External Talent	
Strengths	**Weaknesses**	**Strengths**	**Weaknesses**
Understanding of the ambition level of the organization sponsoring the ITIL implementation	Lacks broad theoretical perspective on ITSM implementations	Understanding of what has worked elsewhere	Understanding of the stakeholder audience of the target client
Able to improvise and adapt ITSM strategy to meet resistance	Lack of external credibility to break-through resistance	Collateral from previous engagements	When you have a hammer everything looks like a nail
High level of commitment to the end solution	This is a one-off project so potential opportunities, roadblocks and alternatives are usually unidentified	Strong theoretical understanding of implementations (Certifications of methods, techniques and best practices)	Tendency to rely on less experienced talent during implementation, compensated by methods and techniques

In-House Talent		External Talent	
Strengths	**Weaknesses**	**Strengths**	**Weaknesses**
High level of knowledge internalization as process progresses	Takes longer to implement due to learning curve	Bring energy and enthusiasm to the task that improves success of the implementation	The ITSM implementation is seen as an 'engagement' with a focus on sign-off results and there is often insufficient attention to coagulation of the results in the longer-term

Table B1

Both approaches can bring success, but in order to do so, both need to compensate for their own limitations. The key to success is when we come to the realization that our designs and our collateral carry the baggage of our own perspectives. While the in-house implementation tends to believe that their situation is unique, the consultant tends to see generic collateral as a trump card. Both are equally right and both are equally wrong, but as we will see, the consultancy approach is less likely to be successful, although not for the reasons you might expect.

The root-cause for underachievement by consultant-lead engagements is over-dependence on collateral as a substitute for learning. The problem is not the collateral itself, which is often of high quality, but the fact that collateral has been given an importance beyond its usefulness. Collateral needs to be understood and internalized by the receiving party before it can ever be usefully and, more importantly, sustainably deployed.

Often the root-cause for underachievement by in-house teams is that they never properly understood or internalized the best practice itself and thereafter, without proper guidance or proper education, embarked on a perilous journey much like Christopher Columbus who, while a successful and famous explorer, remained convinced up until his death that his discoveries where actually on the east-coast of Asia. Columbus traveled but never exactly knew where he was in the grand scheme of things.

Many in-house projects almost entirely entrust their best practice training to a series of ITIL Foundations courses. This is particularly troubling given the limitations of ITIL Foundations training. As I have tried to explain to audiences for years, when we first created the ITIL Foundations, it was an ITIL Essentials aid aimed at interested bystanders within the former Dutch PTT Telecom organization (now KPN) to get greater understanding of the ITIL processes. In this way, 'the cook, cleaner and chauffeur', could all be part of the great ITIL journey. Smart commercial thinking by EXIN turned the essentials into ITIL Foundations, probably the most successful commercial phenomena within the best practices community; however, while extremely useful, the ITIL Foundations course is clearly not an adequate preparation for ITIL implementation.

Having said this, the strength and focus of the external consultants will usually yield results faster. These results will often be fleeting. The in-house project usually has a greater chance of sustainable success, not because it *is* unique, but because it *believes* it is unique. The team will have to exert extra effort to create its own collateral, often with limited external support, and this creation process in itself enables the team to internalize the journey in all of the individuals who participate.

Both approaches will benefit from a well thought-out education strategy:

- The externally lead project will benefit from education that enables the target audience to co-create an implementation experience.
- The internal project will benefit from education that enables them to assimilate the necessary knowledge of best practices.

Education is therefore an important tool in assisting both in-house and consultant-lead implementations to achieve greater success.

Education generally has three components to it:
- content (knowledge) – the best practices and their context
- training – application of the best practices in a specific context (a tool or a scenario)
- forming competence – creating the confidence, the enthusiasm and the courage within individuals to adopt best practices

The ITIL world today is over reliant on content and training, and has generally given inadequate attention to the aspect of competence forming. For successful and sustainable implementations, I would argue that the forming element is almost as important as the content. Eleanor Roosevelt once said, "Maturity occurs when we turn the mirror we use to view ourselves as we are today into a window, to see what is possible and what we can become."

Seeing our own transformation as a key to the success of organizational transformation is crucial. The external consultants tend to play this down because they often haven't experienced this type of transformation themselves (so don't recognize its importance); it also interferes with their ability to deploy objective collateral to a subjective situation. In-house teams are usually unaware of the underlying forming process they are going through themselves, as they are focused on the business objective of implementing best practices.

A useful analogy here is suggested to us by Karl E. Weick (Weick, 1995), that much of what happens in organizational transformation is less about our intent and more about improvisation. To illustrate the difference, I am sure that many readers would appreciate a comparison between managing an organizational transformation and managing improvised theatre.

We both start with a semblance of a script, which in our case is usually based on the best practices. We have actors, but we are not sure of their capabilities. We have an audience that we are playing to (in fact a different one every day). The actors themselves are often typecast before coming to us and this new script will test them; they will have to overcome their own sense of stage-fright. Taken together this means that every performance is actually unique even though the configuration items (stage, props, tools, and venue) and the script essentially remain the same. In fact, there are companies like the Swiss based Sparks[1] that have built a consulting and training business around this concept of management as improvised theatre.

The difference between the performing arts and our own line of business is best illustrated by a quote from Peter Vail. "One mistake the arts would never make is to presume that a part or role can be exactly specified independent of the performer, yet this is the idea that has dominated work organizations for the past 100 years." (Vail, 1991)

When we understand this concept fully we can then start to appreciate the limitations of collateral that are not really intended to enable actors to perform better, but are more often unfiltered regurgitations of someone else's experience.

Given this perspective Weick offers us a few observations regarding organizational design that enable us to make more effective use of education as a tool.

Let us examine a few of these insights:

1. Environments change more rapidly than do organizations
2. An effective organization has few crises and inefficiencies
3. An organization design is a blueprint
4. The purpose of organizational design is to facilitate decision-making
5. Organization designs produce order through intention
6. Organization design affects managerial ability
7. Managerial action is individual
8. People impose controls, and activities are the objects of control

I wonder how many readers are nodding in agreement with these insights.

Now the crux of Weick's observations is that each of these insights we believe(d) to be true are actually myths.

---

[1] www.sparks-training.ch

As we will see shortly, each of these truths that have dominated so much organizational design work are defective. So, in turn, any organization design that is based on these myths is probably doomed to underachievement, if not to failure.

Many of the education strategies around the transformation are also based on these myths, and so consequently do not well serve the people involved in the transition.

Educational strategies that mirror these organizational design myths:

- tend to focus on content and training as opposed to forming
- tend to be heavily front-loaded at the start of the project
- tend to focus on transferring insights from the consultant instead of enabling the target audience to acquire insights

When we view a typical educational strategy derived from traditional thinking it looks like figure B1.

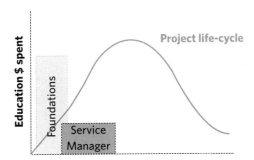

Figure B1

The front-end is loaded with ITIL Foundations training that is intended to train people in the important concepts contained within ITIL and also to create awareness of the need for change.

The service manager training is usually conducted up-front as a kick-off, but before the roles in the new organization have been assigned.

In many situations, most of the education budget has been allocated in this first phase, with only incidental training scheduled for later on in the process.

The effects of this deployment influence the success of the project in the manner visualized in figure B2.

After an initial phase of confusion as the actors grapple with the intent of the project, people get on-board. There is a significant improvement in the

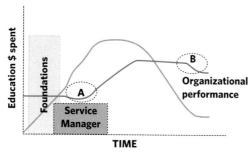

Figure B2

organizational performance as the actors rally around processes designed by the project team.

After the project is complete, people leave the organization to ply their newfound talents elsewhere and the external consultants leave; the organizational focus decreases. The enthusiasm for continual improvement diminishes and usually the organization, now tired, fails to achieve its potential and declares victory on a limited sub-set of the original goals or starts to revert back to the original state.

Many of us will recognize the difference between conceptual learning and internalized learning. I have often watched a master at work -whether it was woodwork at school (a particular personal trauma of mine) or a potter at his wheel. In such cases I have fully understood what they were doing while they were doing it, but this understanding never helped me come close to achieving their products. In the same way I observe students in a class listening and understanding everything I tell them about my experiences, but this does not mean that my experiences actually become *their* experiences. The analogy I use is one of a block of ice. If I give you a block of ice, it would be very tangible. You could see it; you could hold it and you could feel the cold pass through your hands, freezing your entire body. However, once you leave and make your way home, the ice starts to melt and by the time you have reached home all you have are cold wet hands and the ice that was once so concrete is no longer solid, but has disappeared into a vague puddle.

So how should we view education as part of the ITIL implementation process? Let us return to Weick and examine his insights in the context of an ITIL implementation.

> **Do environments change more rapidly than organizations?** For most organizations the answer is clearly no! When I worked at GE and HP both organizations changed their organizations comprehensively at least once a year and within that year a myriad of minor changes would

also complement the grand design. This means that **the stakeholders and sponsors of our implementation will change more often than the underlying need for an ITIL implementation itself.**

An effective organization has few crises and inefficiencies. There is no perfect design for any given situation. The world is too complex for that. However, we can choose organizational designs that are expedient or more useful to achieving our goals for any given moment of time. Organizational design has always been a consequence of compromise – of choosing the shortcomings that you can live with most easily to better achieve your goals. Weick suggests that the true situation is that: **an effective organization has many crises and inefficiencies and that proper organizational design is successful because it exploits crises and inefficiencies.**

An organization design is a blueprint. This approach is much favored in our line of business, as many have a technical or architectural background. Over the years I have personally found that the internal turbulence of the organization that IT is part of or serves means that every blueprint has a very limited lifespan and needs continual calibration for the new audience that appears following change. I have often referred to our profession as one akin to building sandcastles (Nance, 2004). Each time we complete a magnificent project the organizational tides come in to sweep the results away. My conclusion is that the product of our work is not the sandcastle that might be visible for a moment in time, but the competence we instil to build better sandcastles faster between the tides. Weick suggests that: **an organization design is not a blueprint but in fact a recipe that is continually reconstructed.**

The purpose of organizational design is not to facilitate decision-making. Our obsession with RACI or ARCI diagrams has progressed from guidance to gospel, and what is a useful tool has now often become a religious requirement. The fallacy is that people decide and then they act; in practice many people act and then decide, so decision-making can only be effective when consequences are understood. In this order of things: **the purpose of organizational design is not to facilitate decision-making, but to facilitate interpretation.**

Organization designs produce order through intent. Intent is clearly important, but it is the interpretation of the intent and the attention that actors give to realizing this intent that determines whether or not the implementation will succeed. As Weick would say: **organizational designs produce order through attention.**

Organization design affects managerial ability. Assuming that anyone put in charge of a process will succeed with the right process diagrams, content training and RACI charts is inherently flawed. Building on the concept of casting actors according to talent available to us, we all know that the actors available to us will determine a large part of our success. Even the most accomplished film director cannot overcome poor casting. **So organization design only marginally affects managerial ability, in fact managerial ability affects design.**

Managerial action is individual. In the western cultures, most particularly the US culture, there is a significant expectation assigned to the individual leader and the manager: a strong charismatic individual that listens, analyzes and imposes their will on the organization. This idea has been debunked many times, most effectively in 'Good to Great' (Collins, 2001). The strong charismatic CEO is seldom more effective than a team of potentially more low-key individuals executing a shared plan.

One of my early mentors, Professor Dr. Joop Swieringa, posed the question to every freshman at the Nyenrode Business University in The Netherlands: "Why is it that a management team will unanimously agree on a course of action that none of the individuals actually subscribe to?" An insider account that illustrates this point is afforded us by my former boss, Carly Fiorina. Carly is arguably one of the most charismatic and high profile leaders in corporate America. I know from my own experience that she is a strong, smart and determined personality. She is certainly neither a wimp nor a shrinking violet. Yet in her book, Tough Choices: A Memoir (Fiorina, 2006) she describes intricate exchanges between her and her stakeholders in terms of social interaction. These exchanges show us that sometimes, against her own judgment, she took decisions that made sense within a specific social context, but they were decisions that she didn't actually fully support. **Managerial action is not individual it is social.**

People impose controls and activities are the objects of control. Anyone who has ever visited the Republic of Singapore or indeed my residential town of Greenwich, Connecticut USA would believe that the inhabitants are unruly citizens prone to random acts of civil disobedience. There are signs everywhere, 'don't litter', 'don't skateboard', 'don't let animals out unleashed', 'don't spit out chewing gum on the pavement'. In fact, after careful observation, one can see that the inhabitants put these signs up for visitors; they don't need the signs themselves, nor is there any enforcer pervasively ensuring compliance. The truth is that *ideas impose control*, especially the ideas as to reasoning behind the rules. Understanding and internalizing the intent is critical for adequate enforcement. So it is not the activities themselves that require our control, but the ideas behind them. While this may sound a little like something out of Orwell's book, 1984 (Orwell, 1950) it is actually about helping people understand intent, creating designs that influence that understanding and ideas that develop from that understanding. **People do not impose effective controls and activities are not the objects of effective control. Ideas impose control and therefore ideas about the organizational design need to be the object of influence and control.**

By now I hope that I have convinced you that in order to affect the organizational transformation that will lead to successful implementation of a sustainable ITIL implementation we need to educate differently.

Our education strategy needs to meet the following criteria:

- Teach the best practices content at the right level to the right audience at the right time.
- Create awareness about the transformation process that is substantially different from content and allows people to come to their own conclusions about a need for change.
- Focus on transferring the intent of a role and understanding of the process to the actors (staff) rather than just learning the script (collateral).
- Focus on creating shared experiences to build social cohesion that the managers (directors) and actors (staff) need for sustainable success.

Of course, not all of these issues or considerations can be addressed solely through education, but let us see how a good education strategy can help.

Our overall goal now is to create an education strategy that enables both the transfer of knowledge, as well as accomplishing what the organizational consultant Peter Lijnse refers to as 'turning the key of willingness' (Lijnse, 2007) in our actors.

B.1 Applying implementation best practices to educational strategy

As we can see in figure B3, the use of education needs to be spread over the entire project.

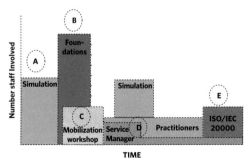

Figure B3

The objective of awareness is to allow people to reflect on their own situation and identify areas of improvement. Some theories refer to this as the phase of being 'consciously incompetent'; 'ITIL Foundations' was never designed to achieve this and is inadequate for the purpose. Instead of using Foundations as an awareness tool, use a simulation tool. Each of the major suppliers has their own version. I have always been partial to Apollo 13 because of its versatility, but any good simulation will serve the same purpose. The simulation can also be used as an educational tool to solidify the process later in the project and to offer an opportunity for actors to reflect on their progress again after the implementation is in full swing.

The true purpose of ITIL Foundations is to offer all of the actors, and indeed the audience, a glimpse of the script. It helps them to understand the specific terms used by ITIL and in what context the terms will be used. This helps them to understand the roles of the actors and the processes they represent.

It is important that the actors get an opportunity to collaborate and to discuss their relative perspectives on the roles and processes that will be enacted. A Mobilization Workshop is a combination of ITIL theory, baselines, assessment and gap analysis. However, the true goal is to facilitate the shared co-creation experience, even while we are introducing the script through established collateral such as the subway maps used by CA.

Now when actors are aware of their shortcomings, understand the intent and have a shared co-created roadmap, they are ready to become 'consciously competent'. Their ability and willingness to learn is enhanced. The Service Manager's courses are essential to all who intend to play a major part in the production. They also need to be ongoing, as there will be attrition both when people perform well and when they are promoted, and also when their ambitions take them outside of the organization. For the more specific typecast roles - the specialist functions in each discipline – a more specific typecast education needs to be deployed: The ITIL Practitioners.

To ensure that the journey is ongoing, new developments in the industry such as ISO/IEC 2000 need to be introduced to the performers in our organization. Best practices are not set in stone but emergent, and the constant review of state-of-the-art practices needs to be instilled in the culture and working practices. New developments are often variations on a theme and the (by now) 'unconsciously competent' actor will pick these up in no time.

Best practice implementation experience suggests that applying educational strategically will, as shown in figures B4 and B5, not only lead to actors who understand their roles and the intent of the processes better, but it will also mean less effort and better results in the overall implementation.

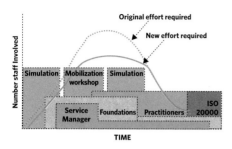

Figure B4

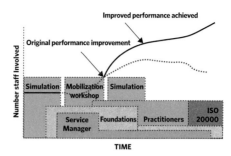

Figure B5

This should not surprise us too much as the difference between this suggested approach and the more traditional approach is that the actors are encouraged to empower themselves. They are *learning* from their own experience as they create their own journey. They are leveraging collateral rather than learning it. Whether the project is wholly internal or consultant-driven, both should benefit from the suggested approach.

When we factor the human elements of intent, understanding and improvisation into the equation, the results improve. It also reminds me of wisdom imparted from Oscar Wilde that I have quoted many times on my own implementation journeys:
"Rules are for the guidance of wise men and the obedience of fools."

As you develop your own educational strategy, know which you are and who 'they' are!

Bibliography

Collins, J. (2001). *Good to Great.* Random House Business Books.
Fiorina, C. (2006). *Touch Choices – A memoir.* Portfolio.
Lijnse, P. (2007, April 2). *Turn the key of willingness.* Calgary, Canada.
Nance, A. (2004). *Castles in the sand – Learning to Embrace Change, the HP story.* Palo Alto: Hewlett Packard Development Company.
Orwell, G. (1950). *1984.* Signet Classics .
Vail, P. (1991). *Management as a Performing Art; New Ideas for a World of Chaotic Change .* Jossey-Bass.
Weick, K. E. (1995). Organizational redesign as improvisation. In H. a. Glick, *Organizational Change and Redesign: Ideas and Insights for improving performance.* Oxford University Press.